FROM ONE
SINGLE
MOTHER
TO ANOTHER

Advice and Encouragement from Someone Who's Been There

SANDRA PICKLESIMER ALDRICH

Regal Books

A Division of Gospel Light Publications
Ventura, California, U.S.A.

Published by Regal Books
A Division of Gospel Light Publications
Ventura, California 93006
Printed in U.S.A.

Library of Congress Cataloging-in-Publication Data

Aldrich, Sandra Picklesimer.
    From one single mother to another / Sandra Picklesimer Aldrich.
        p.   cm.
    Includes bibliographical references.
    ISBN 0-8307-1480-4
    1. Single mothers—United States. 2. Single mothers—United States—Life skills guides. 3. Single mothers—Religious life.
I. Title.
HQ759.915.A43 1991
306.85'6—dc20
                                          91-24666
                                            CIP

Rights for publishing this book in other languages are contracted by Gospel Literature International (GLINT). GLINT also provides technical help for the adaptation, translation, and publishing of Bible study resources and books in scores of languages worldwide. For further information, contact GLINT, Post Office Box 488, Rosemead, California, 91770, U.S.A., or the publisher.

DEDICATION

To my son and daughter, Jay and Holly Aldrich.
Thanks, kiddos, for keeping me from running away
to Tahiti—or Kentucky—at the beginning of
my singlehood and for giving me lots of reasons
to see the joy in each new day.

Your Single Mom
Colorado Springs, CO
April 1991

CONTENTS

ACKNOWLEDGMENTS

D uring those years of trying to find my footing in my new role as a single mother, I gleaned information from other single mothers as they told me of their trials. So, much of what I share here is from them. And in appreciation of the trust they've shown me, I've changed most of their names in these pages to protect their privacy.

But I especially want to thank my sister April Thea Picklesimer for sharing insights from her circumstances. Her encouraging calls always came when I needed them most.

Neither this book nor its predecessor, *Living Through the Loss of Someone You Love*, would have been written without gentle prodding from my dear "family" at Regal Books. Everyone there deserves one of my Kentucky hugs, but several folks went out of their way to show special kindness: Mr. and Mrs. Bill Greig, Jr., Mark Maddox, Kyle Duncan, Linda Holland, Gloria Moss, Susan Adkins—and my editor, Earl Roe.

Each one had an important part in this latest project, but Earl's brotherly concern about my being so tough on myself has been a special gift.

God bless you all.

A Letter from One Single Mother to Another

"Woe is me for my hurt! my wound is grievous: but I said, Truly this is a grief, and I must bear it."
JEREMIAH 10:19, *KJV*

Dear Friend:

The book you are holding is written by this single mom to help and encourage you, another hurting—perhaps newly—single mom. It picks up from where my earlier book on bereavement, *Living Through the Loss of Someone You Love*, leaves off.

I confess I never expected to write either of these books. After all, I was raised to take care of a husband and children. Singlehood and parenting children on my own just weren't part of the deal.

So I've learned far more than I ever wanted to know about being either a widow or a single mother since that December 1982 afternoon when cancer defeated my husband, Don, and spun me into single parenthood.

Know then that, if you're a recent single mom and juggling too many responsibilities, I understand some of what you're dealing with. Much of the spiritual and practical counsel I offer through these pages I've learned myself the hard way—by living through it. But don't worry, I won't try to advise you on how to raise perfect youngsters—I'm still trying to figure out how to do *that* myself. I simply pray you will find in this book encouragement that, in Christ, you and your children *do* have bright tomorrows.

Occasionally, one of my married friends will ask what single parenting is like. Imagine a tightrope strung across a deep gorge. A single mother gingerly walks across the rope, trying to concentrate on the numerous balls she's juggling. Some have labels: "child care" or "work" or "debt" or "health." Perhaps even "rejection" and "custody battles" are included, but always she's worrying about keeping too many balls in the air at the same time.

On each side of the gorge run folks clamoring for her attention—children, parents, bosses, friends. Then one smooth-talking type gestures for her to step off the rope and join him. At places where the rope dips close to the ground on which he stands, it would be easy for her to drop all those balls and step onto his stony path. But the mother continues on, looking only at the responsibility coming down toward her hand at the moment, knowing that, if she looks away, she can easily lose her balance.

The Church doesn't always help us keep our balance either. The divorced women especially have my sympathy. When my husband died, everyone hovered around me, whispering, "Oh, you poor dear." But when one of my sisters and several of my friends divorced—one even did so to protect her daughter from sexual abuse—they were treated like lepers.

Sometimes it seems as though many churches forgive anything but divorce. Recently one of my friends told me about a gal who was taken by the elbow and "escorted" out of a communion service by an elder the week after her divorce became final.

Christian compassion compels us also to reach out in love to another category of women who are trying desperately to raise their children alone—those unmarried mothers who have bravely rejected the option of abortion. They have determined instead that with God's help—and hopefully with that of their local church—to raise their children themselves.

And when it comes to this business of combining singlehood

and motherhood, unmarried moms find themselves walking the same tightrope and juggling the same balls as do we widows and divorcees. So welcome to the world of the single moms, ladies!

One of the biblical responsibilities of the Church is the care of "orphans and widows" (Jas. 1:27). Today, that responsibility often translates into providing emotional and financial help for single women and their children—no matter how they arrived at that status—and this concern is one ball that the Church dares not drop.

And before we go any further, I need to get one of my pet peeves out of the way: people who constantly refer to single-parent families as "broken homes." Many of us feel that through God's help and a great deal of personal effort, our homes are healed, even if—as in my case—the healing didn't come overnight.

* * *

In those first, early days of my singlehood, I couldn't look ahead to where we are now. While thinking—and worrying—about my single-parenting role, all I could do was look to the examples of strong women from the Bible and from my own family.

I wanted to be like Anna of Luke 2:36—the one who had served in the Temple for most of her adult life. But, unlike Anna, I couldn't withdraw from the world—economics wouldn't let me.

I thought, too, of Molly Pitcher, the woman who carried water to wounded and dying men during the Revolutionary War. Her real name was Molly Ludwig Hays, but her chosen responsibility gave her the nickname that stuck ever after.

During one particularly fierce battle, she saw her husband fall beside the cannon he was firing. She ran to his side, not to cradle him in her arms, but to take his place and to fire the cannon for him!

I wanted to be that type of woman! But I learned early that our own strength alone can't conquer all situations.

My great-grandmother Mintie Farley often related her early memories of the craziness surrounding the War Between the States (Northern textbooks *insist* on calling it "The Civil War"). She remembered that all the men in their little settlement were gone to war, leaving their wives and children alone on the Kentucky hillside farms.

The Yankees—okay, the Union Army—had stolen everything they could, including the family's lone milk cow. But one late afternoon horsemen stormed into the yard, demanding the last of their food. Her mother, Stacee Collins, started to argue, but the major merely pointed his pistol at her head and said it would be a shame to have to kill her in front of the children. She gave the soldiers the food.

Over the years—and long after my great-grandmother's death—the story was retold so much and became so real to me that I could have reported the color of the major's hair. As I'd express my indignation, my grandmother Mama Farley would say, "Honey, there are some things in life that all you can do with 'em is bear 'em."

So learning to bear singleness with grace didn't come overnight. I've made mistakes along the way and exhausted a few of my friends who couldn't help me through my pain.

I'm much stronger now, but it's taken prayer and personal pep talks to get there. For the past five years, I've had above my desk a quotation from Helen Keller: "Life is either a daring adventure or nothing."

In my own battle with low self-esteem, I've learned that negative thoughts often produce negative actions which, in turn, produce negative results. Psychologists call this phenomenon "the self-fulfilling prophecy."

Remember saying years ago, "Why bother studying for this test? I'm just going to flunk it anyway." And sure enough, you did flunk it? Well, we can sabotage our future in the same way, if we're not careful.

From those early, frightening years I'm now seeing singlehood as a wonderful adventure. Because of Jesus, if we'll accept His help, we do have the hope and assurance that we can be good single mothers.

So go ahead and smile. Better days *are* ahead for you and your children.

Meanwhile, let me take your hand, and share with you some of the things I've learned along the way.

Cordially,

Sandra

ONE

IF I CAN DO IT, YOU CAN, TOO

*"I can do everything through him
who gives me strength."*
PHILIPPIANS 4:13

My daughter, Holly, was in the third grade when she came home one day in tears. One of the room mothers had handed out printed directions to a special event and said, "Take these home to your families."

Then she'd glanced at Holly and said, "Sorry. I mean 'to your moms.'"

In our Michigan kitchen, I put my arm around my eight-year-old. "Holly, we are still a family," I said. "We're just a family of *three* now."

She leaned against me in relief. That was a turning point for both of us.

That incident, along with others, made me realize that, if we were going to survive as a family, we'd have to fight a few emotional battles along the way. And the only way my kiddos could develop their own strength was by watching me.

Overnight We Become Single Moms
But We Survive Just the Same

Yet when my husband, Don, died in 1982, my own strength faded. How could I handle all the things single mothers had to do? I had gone from my father's authority to my husband's. And even though I'd taught in a Detroit suburban school and had handled numerous professional responsibilities, I knew nothing about paying bills, budgeting, balancing a checkbook, doing home maintenance or repairing a car.

And how could I raise two children to be healthy adults without their father? How could I teach my 10-year-old son to be a man? Neither Don's family nor mine offered a close-at-hand male relative who could provide the father-figure Jay would need.

So I worried and prayed about that a lot in those first years after becoming a single mom. I kept Jay in church, and trusted that those couple of hours each week would provide him with glimpses of what Christian manhood was like.

Nine years have passed since his dad's death, and Jay's grown up with a mother, a sister and a neutered cat. Yet today he is a healthy, manly young man.

We Win Some and We Lose Some
But That's How We Learn

So what have I learned along the way that I feel genuinely helped me and will also help you? I have no pat answers or perfect solutions—and beware anyone who says they have— but I can tell you what has worked—or didn't work—for me and for the other single mothers who shared their experiences with me. And remember, whatever successes and achievements came our way were rarely the result of any innate wisdom that we had. As a rule, they came about because of much grace on God's part and much trial-and-error on our part.

None of us women raising children alone has identical concerns or faces identical circumstances, so as you read our stories, select those ideas and options that you feel hold promise of benefit for you and ignore the rest.

Whatever else I am—a former wife and teacher, a widow and a single mom, a writer and an editor—my foremost goal in life is to be God's woman. So, in this chapter, I begin with some spiritual concerns that are vitally important to all of us, along with some practical matters that we single moms face in common. Then in each succeeding chapter, I will discuss a particular issue that concerns us a lot and will offer a smorgasbord of various do's and don'ts as I go along. But first things first, right?

We Can Draw Encouragement from Scripture

I'm originally from Harlan County, Kentucky, and proud of my strong mountain heritage. But those who know me best are aware that even as I set my Kentucky jaw, I still occasionally struggle with feelings of inadequacy. In the past, I've even

◆◆

In John 11—the raising of Lazarus from the dead....I'm fascinated that Jesus had to say, "*Lazarus*, come out." I'm convinced that, since He is Life, every grave would have given up its dead if He had shouted a mere "Come out!"

◆◆

fought a tendency to call myself stupid—especially when I didn't get the hang of something as quickly as I had hoped or a boss had wanted.

In those moments, I played all my mental tapes of every mistake I've ever made. But over the years, I've learned that I'm not the only single mother who's trying to fit the ball of good self-esteem into the collection she's already juggling.

And I'm working on my low self-esteem, but that feeling of being woefully inadequate was especially strong early in my singlehood, so I often turned to the Bible for encouragement. Learning that Old Testament women such as Deborah, Ruth and Esther also faced impossible situations and won—with God's help—strengthened me greatly. Soon I was personalizing everything I read in the Scriptures.

One of my favorite accounts of a miracle is in John 11—the raising of Lazarus from the dead. Mary and Martha of Bethany sent word to Jesus that their brother, Lazarus, was very ill.

Jesus deliberately stalled, until He heard that His friend had died. When He finally arrived in Bethany, He went to the grave and told the men standing nearby to roll away the stone.

Then He said in a loud voice, "Lazarus, come out!" (John 11:43).

I'm fascinated that Jesus had to say, "*Lazarus,* come out." I'm convinced that, since He is Life, every grave would have given up its dead if He had shouted a mere "Come out!"

When Lazarus emerged from the tomb, he was still bound in the grave clothes. Jesus then said to those standing nearby—surely with their mouths hanging open—"Take off the grave clothes and let him go" (v. 44).

How's that again? The One who raised a man from the dead was asking mere humans to roll away stones and untie grave clothes?

Yes, because He wanted to make a visual point: *Do what you can and leave the outcome with the Lord.* In other words, do what is humanly possible and leave the miraculous stuff to Him.

Even now I'm relieved at the implication here for single mothers: Our Lord will give us the strength to juggle all *our* responsibilities. In faith, we have to do what we can do—and not give up.

It's like the old adage says, "Pray as though everything depends on God, and work as though everything depends on you."

Try Claiming Isaiah 54:5 as Your Own

This reference traditionally has been called "the widow's verse," but it's for all single women: "For your Maker is your husband—the Lord Almighty is his name."

I drew special comfort from the message of this verse because I'd never made a major decision by myself before and was terrified that a wrong choice would jeopardize my children's future. I prayed about everything—large and small.

Not only did I get the direction I needed, but I learned to trust my common sense, too.

When our sunroom ceiling began leaking after a severe ice storm, I took an entire evening to think about it on paper. First I listed why I should choose simple repair. Then I listed all the reasons for replacing the entire roof.

In my prayer, I reminded the Lord of His promise to be my husband—not for His benefit but for my own—then added, "Lord, husbands worry about roofs. So I'm going to sleep and let You figure it out."

The next morning, I awakened with the thought that the smartest thing for me to do was to let my favorite carpenter not only redo the roof, but also increase the slant so ice wouldn't collect in the corner again.

Think Angels and Invoke Our Lord's Protection

In Luke 4:10, God said He would put angels over us to protect us. But it wasn't until I was in Israel that I decided He wasn't teasing.

I'd wandered into the modern area near the hotel where our church group was staying. Dressed in a straw hat and slacks outfit, I walked for perhaps an hour. Then as I sat down on a low wall to get my bearings so I could head back to the hotel, I discovered I was unwelcome. Someone threw small stones at me from behind a nearby fence.

Oh, cute, I thought. Here I am, an American woman alone on the streets of a Middle Eastern country. So I told myself that perhaps the stones were being thrown by an obnoxious kid who would take great pleasure in any fear I displayed.

But I realized that if I'd tried all day, I probably couldn't have come up with anything more thoughtless. I took a deep breath.

"Well, Lord, this isn't the brightest thing I've done," I told Him. "But I thank You for the promise that angels are watching over me.

"Now I'd like one special angel to walk beside me. And since angels can take any form they want, I'd like him to be big and ugly—and visible to anyone whose heart is evil."

I imagined my personal angel as about 6'8" and 290

pounds with his longish brown hair held back with a don't-mess-with-me bandanna. I even nicknamed my angel "Buddy." Then I stood up and, ignoring the stones falling around me, walked confidently all the way back to the hotel with my escort Buddy beside me.

When I returned to the States I told Jay and Holly about the situation, adding the usual admonishment that we aren't to test God by foolishly taking risks. Ten-year-old Holly quickly took to the idea of angels' care.

So when we moved to New York a couple of years later, she asked, "If Buddy's with us in the hotel, who's gonna watch the truck with our furniture?"

So I created Buddy's twin brother, "Buford." I described how he would stand outside the truck, leaning against it and cleaning his fingernails with a pocket knife.

If any kids snooped around the truck, he'd quietly come around the side of the vehicle and say, "I reckon you boys better go someplace else."

Being a Kentuckian, I'm sure *Southern* angels watched over us during that move. The theology here may be shaky, but Buddy and Buford helped my frightened young daughter—and her mother—to sleep well just the same.

When We Forget Worry and Pray a Lot
We See God Answer in Many Ways

Philippians 4:19 is a verse I claimed early as a single mother: "But my God shall supply all your need according to his riches in glory by Christ Jesus" (*KJV*).

Many times I tested that promise and occasionally challenged Him with "even *this* need, God?"

Gradually, I learned He hadn't overlooked anything. As I learned to pray about every challenge and decision, He answered in marvelous ways.

Sometimes He used friends to show me how to change the oil in the car or to balance the checkbook. Sometimes He encouraged me through a glorious sunset and with the constant thought that He hadn't left me alone.

But most of all He helped me grow, and, as I did, I learned much about myself and even more about my heavenly Father.

Maintaining Our Family Routines
Provides Us with Structure

Structure often gets us over the rough spots. So having a set time for meals, homework and chores adds needed organization to our schedules. And if single parents need anything in their routine, it's regular Scripture reading.

For years, we've read the Bible after weekday dinners and kept track of our prayer requests in a notebook. Guests, including any of Jay's and Holly's friends who happen to be over for dinner, are invited to join us.

One evening Holly's friend, Jessica, and Jay's German friend, Till, were with us. As we finished our meat loaf, Jay read several of our favorite psalms.

◆◆

Being a single mom is hard work. Naturally, we'd love to have a pat on the shoulder occasionally, but looking for that praise takes energy that is better used in tending to the duties at hand.

◆◆

I then explained that it was our custom to take turns praying, and that Till was welcome to join us.

He nervously replied, "But I've never prayed in English!"

"Then pray in German," I said. "You're talking to God, not to us. But you don't have to pray aloud if you don't want to. You do whatever makes you feel comfortable."

So Jay opened the prayer time, followed by Jessica and Holly. I was all set to close the prayers when Till hesitantly began to pray. In his first timid words, I caught the word "Deutsch" and knew he was telling the Lord that I'd said he should pray in German.

Gradually, his timidity slipped away, and he began earnestly to talk to God. Even though I couldn't understand the words, I understood the emotion—and felt the thankfulness that welled up within his prayer.

We would have missed a special blessing that evening if we had set aside our family routine because of guests.

We Must Be Realistic in Our Expectations of Others

Most of us learned a long time ago that we can't expect others to be all we need them to be. Here's what we've learned the hard way:

Don't Expect Others to Do Everything for You

I remember one young widow who demanded that the men of the church answer her every call for help. If her car tires needed air or if her house windows were dirty, she called on the churchmen to assist her. When they balked—after all, most of them didn't do windows for their *own* wives!—she complained to the pastor, saying the church was supposed to take care of its widows.

That's true, but only to a point. The instructions in James 1:27 direct the Church to provide for their shelter and food, but not for taking over work they can—and should—do for themselves.

Don't Expect Others to Take on Your Hurt

Even though it's been almost 12 years since her divorce, Jan still holds a grudge against a woman in her church who didn't respond in the way Jan had felt she should have.

In great detail, Jan describes the Wednesday night service when her husband handed her the car keys, said, "Who are we trying to kid?" and walked out.

In that moment, she knew their struggling marriage was over. Numb, she sat through the rest of the service, wanting to give him enough time to walk the few blocks home and to pack his suitcase.

After the service, the woman sitting behind her asked if everything was all right. With tears running down her cheeks, Jan blurted out that she was facing a divorce.

"Then the woman patted my arm, said God would be with me and went home to *her* husband!" Jan says.

Sure, it would have been wonderful if the woman had

wrapped her in a hug and said, "Oh, Honey!" but she didn't.

If we're going to think, *it's not fair,* and be hurt every time someone fails to provide what we think we need, we're going to be hurting a lot. Other people have their own problems, too, and they can't take on ours any more than we can take on theirs.

Welcome the help when it comes, but don't demand it. By looking at our situation realistically, we can get through it with less trauma.

Don't Expect Others to Appreciate What You Do

Being a single mom is hard work. Naturally, we'd love to have a pat on the shoulder occasionally, but looking for that praise takes energy that is better used in tending to the duties at hand. Remember, the ancient Greeks didn't award the prize to the winner who crossed the finish line first, but to the one who finished first *with his torch still burning!*

Besides, other folks don't always realize just how much we're doing, anyway. I learned that in 1968, when a relative and I drove to Kentucky to bring my grandparents, Papa and Mama Farley, and my Aunt Adah back to Michigan.

An eight-hour drive was ahead of us, so my grandmother had an enormous lunch perched next to her on the front seat. On top of the picnic hamper she balanced a bunch of bananas, then settled her cane comfortably against her thigh, ready to begin the trip.

In the late 1960s, Interstate 75 wasn't complete yet, and numerous detours forced us to wind around the southern hills on dangerously curving stretches of asphalt. Topping one more hill, we discovered that a rock slide had covered the road.

The relative got out of the car after hastily putting the gear into park. Then, just as he climbed onto the rock pile to survey the situation, the car stalled and began to roll backward.

I was in the backseat wedged between Aunt Adah and Papa, but it was up to me to reach the brake. In that instant, I threw myself over the seat, knocking the lunch to the floor as I scrambled to stomp onto the brakes.

When I got the car stopped, it was already several feet beyond the asphalt. And beyond that was a 500-foot drop into the ravine below.

With the car safely braked again, I released my breath and then looked at Mama Farley. Surely she had some praise for the quick action on my part that had saved the four of us from severe injury—if not death.

But she merely glanced at me as she picked up the scattered lunch. Then she muttered, "You smashed the bananas."

Don't Expect Others to Be There for You Always

Even as I was trying to learn how to juggle all my new responsibilities alone, my dear friends Dick and Rose Keilhacker completed plans to move to California. On the Sunday evening before they left, we said good-bye in my kitchen.

I tried to be brave, but my tears were threatening as I hugged Rose. Then as I turned toward Dick, he gave me such a sorrowful look that I absolutely lost it. All I could do was sob against his shoulder.

My rare display of public emotion created an awkward moment for all of us, but I couldn't stop. Two of my dearest friends were leaving for the end of the world, and I was sure I'd never see them again.

When I finally got myself together, we were all embarrassed enough that I determined inwardly I'd never let such a scene occur again, no matter how much I cared about the ones who were leaving. Ironically, nine years later now, business often takes me to southern California, and I stay with Rose and Dick whenever I can. I didn't lose them forever, after all.

Even though I had felt at the time that my little raft had just been set adrift, it forced me to stop depending on my friends and start searching for my own strength—and that of the Lord. Over time, I found it, too.

Here's What We Must Avoid For Our Emotional Health

Avoid Jealousy and Envy

Jealousy wastes precious energy, but it took me awhile to learn that important lesson.

At a business meeting, a man mentioned that his wife had given a luncheon for several of the ladies from their church. The table was set with crystal and china while the stereo played quietly. Each woman had rushed into the house but had been quickly soothed and put at ease by the setting in which they found themselves.

"She created a haven for them," he said casually.

I couldn't comment since I was so envious. Sure, she could provide a haven; she was a stay-at-home wife, who had the luxury of concentrating on her main job—that of taking care of a husband and children.

Her days were her own. She could attend Bible study groups, shop at her convenience, bathe in the afternoon and look stunning for her husband—who paid the bills, talked to her and helped her discipline their children. She wasn't having to juggle all those duties and tensions all by herself.

I confess that I can't tell you one other thing that went on at the meeting.

Now when such situations occur, I remind myself I had my turn at those activities, but I chose to leave all that behind when I left my calm life in Michigan and moved to New York to become an editor. I *chose* this life-style.

True, I didn't choose to be single, but I did choose to raise my children alone, and I did choose to change careers in midlife after having taught high schoolers for 15 years.

Taking a get-tough attitude with myself helps me put things in proper perspective.

Avoid Hurtful Fantasizing

Even though I've come a long way since that time, I still have moments of feeling very much alone. Last Christmas, Jay, Holly and I attended "A Colorado Christmas"—an energetic musical with the thin plot a family gathering for Christmas, singing joyful songs and expressing their love for each other without the emotional baggage.

The show was usually given as part of a dinner package, so even our matinee audience was seated at large round tables. In the final moments before the curtain went up, waitresses hurried between the tables, delivering soft drinks.

When the show started, I was delighted by the high energy of the performers who sang and danced as though they were having a wonderful time. Then, during one particularly tender holiday song, I started to cry, feeling very much alone—even though Jay and Holly were sitting on either side of me.

Just then the man across the table pulled his arm back toward his wife. My tears increased as I realized he was going to put his arm around her and give her shoulders a little squeeze.

How fortunate his wife is, and how wonderful of him to do that. My thoughts were moving faster than the man's arm.

At last, with his arm all the way back, he reached for his soft drink—instead of his wife!

I laughed aloud at myself as another of life's realities brought me back to earth and shattered one more of my fantasies.

You Help Yourself and Your Family
When You Help Others

I realized early that I have a tendency to compare myself to others, so the trick for me was to get those comparisons going in the right direction. By reaching out to others, Jay, Holly and I quickly learned to count what we had left instead of what we had lost.

That first Thanksgiving alone, I decided I wasn't going to cook for the usual mob of relatives. And I wasn't going to accept any of the invitations we received. I knew myself well enough to know that being with complete families would only intensify my feelings of loss.

So I called the local Salvation Army and asked if we could help serve dinner. Providing that small service to others helped me far more than I expected it to. And afterwards, the three of us went away with a special feeling of peace.

The day had its humorous moments, too. I'd told Jay and Holly to dress warmly that morning, since the dinner would be served in the gymnasium of a little church. I also told them not to wear their nicest clothes, as I didn't want us to look as though we were condescendingly "doing our good deed" for the year. They apparently followed my instructions too well.

After we had served everyone else, we sat down to eat with our own filled plates. Just as we lifted our heads from prayer, a photographer from the local paper stepped through the doorway. He surveyed the room, spotted my blond youngsters, smiled and came over.

"I'm from the local paper, and we're doing a story on families having dinner at the Salvation Army," he said. "May I take your picture? This will be a great shot—you and your kids."

I panicked. "Oh, no! We're volunteers. We've been serving dinner to the others."

He smiled gently. "It's okay. Everybody needs a little help now and then."

"But we're volunteers," I insisted. "We came to help."

An older gentleman at the next table had been watching the scenario with interest.

"You can take *my* picture," he said. "I won't make as pretty a one as the youngins, but I'll smile fer you."

The photographer shrugged and snapped one shot of the man before moving to the other side of the room. I decided that next year I'd let the kids wear their nicest sweaters.

Being Willing to Make Changes Opens Us to a Newness of Life

Try New Approaches and Be Pleasantly Surprised

Most single moms hear at least occasionally, "Daddy didn't do it that way," whether we're frying potatoes or cleaning out the garage.

When Melanie's children said things like that to her, she used to remind them, "Well, Daddy's not here!" But she soon realized such a retort only deepened the gloom. Finally she forced herself to ask them to show her "how Daddy would do this."

To her delight, Jimmy, her 10-year-old son, remembered how to pour the gasoline into the lawn mower tank without splashing. Soon she was asking Jimmy how *he* would tackle a task.

Take an Occasional Risk and Grab *This* Moment

We can become so worried about the future—paying bills,

making friends, finding a new environment—that we miss the joy of *this* moment. This concern was an especially tough area for me to deal with because I'd always had my security blankets—friends, family, familiar environment— wrapped tightly around me.

But once I forced myself to take little risks, even to changing my basic wardrobe color from the pinks I used to wear to the deep purples I'd always loved, I discovered a heart for adventure.

That realization quickly translated into having fun with my young children, including garbage-bag tobogganing near their grandparents' home. I even took to carrying a box of oversized bags in the trunk for such impromptu romps.

Even a walk in the woods became an adventure. And looking back now, we recognize that our favorite memories from those early years of adjustment are in the unplanned events—the trips to the cider mills or art fairs—not the trips we overplanned for weeks.

Look for the Silver Lining and Enjoy New Experiences

When I was married, Sunday afternoons revolved around football. If I wanted to invite someone for dinner, they had to like football. If I suggested we visit relatives, we had to leave either well before or immediately after the game.

Now these many years later, I confess that, while I still miss my husband, I don't miss football one bit.

As I reclaimed those fall and winter Sunday afternoons, I started looking for things Jay, Holly and I could do together. Museums, plays and orchestras quickly filled the time that had once belonged to football.

Those activities were some of our choices for a Sunday afternoon; they may not be yours. The point is that, depending on your tastes, budget and the ages of your children, do whatever appeals to you as a family. Maybe visiting with friends and relatives is more to your liking, or taking in a matinee or going to the zoo or whatever.

If you're outdoor types, you've got Sunday driving, hiking, biking and romping in the park, as well as enjoying skating, sledding and all the rest of those cold-weather sports when the temperature drops and the snow starts falling. Indulge and enjoy!

Analyze and Adjust and Celebrate in New Ways

Altering the way we've always celebrated holidays is often the smartest way to handle the pain.

Just after we moved to Colorado Springs, I had lunch with Arlyene Ballard, my realtor and new friend who was wading through the pain of an unwanted divorce.

As she sipped her diet cola, she said, "I remember a guy in our office who said nobody invited him to their Christmas parties after his divorce. The holiday is still four months away, and already I'm wondering what I'm going to do."

I shrugged. "That's easy. You and your kiddos are coming to my place for Christmas dinner."

She shook her head. "I can't do that. There're five of us."

I insisted I was cooking and that if she didn't come for dinner, she'd have to come for leftovers.

Finally she accepted, but only after she insisted we go to her place for Thanksgiving. Suddenly her eyes sparkled at the thought of filling her home again.

Within a few weeks, her guest list consisted of an interesting group of single parents and their children that she teasingly called "The Lost and Found Gang." We all hit it off so well that I invited *all* of them to my home for Christmas.

The Lost and Found Gang is now at the core of my social circle. And all because Arlyene and I were willing to analyze our situations and adjust to a new way of doing things.

Let Down Your Hair and Be a Kid Again, Too

Karen's two children constantly argued over a small blue pillow in the family room. Then she saw teddy bears on sale—soft and fluffy—with tummies just the size of that old blue pillow. She picked out a brown one for her son and a white one for her daughter.

Then just as she turned away with her carefully chosen selections, another white bear—this one with a floppy arm—caught her eye. He was imperfect; no one would buy him. Suddenly, with a surge of kinship, she bought him and named him Ralph.

Many nights, after her children had gone to bed, she sat on the sofa, watched the dying fire and hugged her broken bear. Anyone who's met her in the last few years can't imagine that scene, but maybe she's stronger now because she allowed herself those evenings of hugging a fluffy bear.

Dare to Dare and Do Something Different

Peggy's week in her blue-suit office world had been rough. Now Saturday's chores loomed; it was raining and both her kids had colds. She pulled on her sweatshirt, then noticed she had it on backward. She sighed and started to turn the logo to the front.

Suddenly she grinned at her mirrored reflection and turned her sweat pants inside out before she tugged them on. Then she pulled her hair into a top knot and tied it with a pair of her daughter's lavender tights.

Not only did she feel appropriately dressed for the gloomy morning, but she still occasionally gives in to other tension-relieving "weird days."

Sometimes we have to force ourselves out of our ruts. When things start to close in on Darlene, she takes her children for a walk or, in bad weather, to the mall. Their assignment is to see how many different sounds they can identify. The idea is to do something different—and something fun.

Are you one of those who has to have things "just so"? I used to be. But when the New York editorial job offer came, and we moved into a small condo, the cost of living was so high on the East Coast that I couldn't afford wallpaper right away. So we slapped paint on the walls and moved in.

Within a couple of days of unpacking our boxes, I had hung—with dozens of straight pins—several Amish and Southern quilts to add brightness to the rooms. Then on the awkward wall next to the stairs, I hung the scatter rugs my Kentucky grandmother had braided years ago. Only a few of them were unused; most were ones I had wiped my feet on at her backdoor years ago, never dreaming they'd someday move with me to that great end of the world—New York.

When everything was in place, I stood back to admire the splashes of color against the off-white paint. It was magnificent! What I originally meant as a temporary measure quickly became my personal decorating signature.

Too Often We Wait Too Long
To Take Care of Our Health

This is one of those do-as-I-say-and-not-as-I-do sections. I've always been ready to take care of other people, but I'd never made time to take care of myself.

My weight crept up—and sometimes rushed in—and in the list of priorities, my own health was way down on the bottom. It was, that is, until my intense response to life increased so much that I finally landed myself in an emergency room.

At the time, I was an editor for a Christian magazine in New York and putting in long hours. We desperately needed a secretary to handle the volume of daily mail. My boss had asked the-powers-that-be to get us some help, but the response came down that I was handling the situation just fine.

So September 28 had to happen, sooner or later.

That day, we had our usual intense schedule: Everything was going wrong, deadlines were missed and two readers had called, wanting to talk to someone about decisions they were facing in their own lives. With my grief counseling background, I usually wound up with those calls.

Then just about 4:00 P.M., the overnight courier called, saying they'd lost the artwork for the next issue. I numbly heard only that they would continue to check the warehouse.

Next the accounting department needed me. I got halfway up the stairs when my heart threatened to pound right out of my rapidly tightening chest. All of the invisible balls I'd been juggling that day suddenly clattered at my feet. I couldn't breathe. I gingerly sat down on the step, convinced I was having a heart attack at only 44.

After several minutes of sitting there on the staircase—and praying—my heart stopped pounding enough that I went on to the accounting office.

"Are you all right?" was my friend's quick question.

I nodded. "I'm just tired. It's been a long day."

Quitting time finally arrived, and I called Holly to let her know I'd be late coming home. Then I drove myself directly to the local hospital.

The examining doctor quickly attached me to an EKG (electrocardiograph). Believe me, something about having wires attached to your chest and hooked up to machines that beep every few moments puts life into its proper prospective.

My blood pressure was so dangerously high that the doctor was suddenly more concerned about my having a possible stroke than he was about my having a heart attack. He gave me bitter medicine to hold under my tongue, while I kept wondering about Jay and Holly.

After two hours of running tests, deciding I wasn't having a heart attack after all and bringing my blood pressure down to the high end of normal range, the doctor gave me the name of two heart specialists for follow-up examinations.

Then he said, "Tell me about your life."

I gave him a wry smile. "Not much to tell. I'm a widow, raising two teens alone and putting in 12- to 16-hour days on the job."

He nodded. "Want me to admit you for a few days just so you can catch your breath?"

I shook my head. "Nah. I'll sleep better in my own bed," I said. "But I promise to stay home from work tomorrow and see the specialist as soon as he can take me."

He let me go then. And the moment I walked out that hospital door, I mentally left New York, knowing it was just a matter of time until I tried to take back the control of my life.

Letting Ourselves Laugh Again
Is the Best Kind of Medicine

Giving ourselves permission to laugh again is a tough area for the single mother, especially for those of us who were brought up to take care of others and for whom life was serious stuff.

Proverbs 17:22 tells us that "a cheerful heart is good medicine, but a crushed spirit dries up the bones." But even knowing this truth, it seemed to take *forever* after my husband died before I could allow myself to laugh again.

But laughter did return. And I remember when it happened. One of my relatives was giving an account of some zany experience he had had. I've long forgotten the story he told, but I recall that the corners of my mouth turned up as I listened to him. In that moment, I made a conscious decision to give in to a rib-splitting laugh. And it felt good, as did the release that came with it.

Laughter is not only necessary for special friendship bonding but for good health. We know scientifically that endorphins—a form of the body's own medicine—are released from the brain when we laugh.

Not only does laughter relieve daily tension, but it creates marvelous memories—for us as well as for our youngsters. One of my friends, now close to 90, says she never heard her grandmother laugh and seldom saw her smile—and then only at other adults.

She'd told me that before Jay and Holly turned five, so I asked myself, "If I died now, what would they remember about me?"

I didn't like what seemed the obvious answer: "Don't make a mess!"

I decided right then to look for ways to be more fun to be with. The obvious place was in my attitude, so I reminded myself they were still children and not miniature adults. So not only was it necessary for them to clown around and be silly, but it was okay for me to enjoy their silliness and laugh with them.

Laura's children were four and three when their dad took off. Laughing was the last thing Laura wanted to do, but she also knew she couldn't sit in a darkened house and expect the children to be quiet, too. One evening, in desperation, she draped a blanket over a card table and suggested the children play "Indian."

Within a few minutes, the four-year-old peeked out from under the table and gestured for Laura to join them.

She opened her mouth to say, "No, you just play."

Instead, she said, "Sure!" and thoroughly enjoyed the next 20 minutes being silly with her kids and laughing hilariously at themselves. They had let themselves go, and the cheeriness of their time together was indeed "good medicine" for all of them.

Once More with Feeling

- Draw encouragement and strength from Scripture. Many women in the Bible also faced impossible situations, but came through victoriously.
- Claim Isaiah 54:5, the widow's verse. The reminder that God Himself is our husband helps lighten our load.
- Invoke the Lord's protection and that of His angels.
- Pray—a lot! The Lord helps us, but we have to ask.
- Maintain your family routines. Structure often gets us over the rough spots.
- Be realistic in your expectations of others. No one but the Lord can be all that we need Him to be.
- Know what to avoid. Harboring envy, jealousy, fantasies and the like can only add to our hurt. Longing for what we don't have can cause us to lose the joy of what we do have.
- Try helping others. In doing so, we find peace for ourselves.
- Be willing to make changes. Try new approaches, take occasional risks, dare to do something different and celebrate in new ways. And look for the silver lining—singlehood has its happy moments, too.
- Take care of your health. We're so busy juggling duties and taking care of children that we often forget to be good to ourselves, too.
- And let yourself laugh again. "A cheerful heart is good medicine."

TWO

SO, HOW DO WE HANDLE LONELINESS?

*"But just as he who called you is holy,
so be holy in all you do; for it is written:
'Be holy, because I am holy.'"*
1 PETER 1:15-16

As I entered my second year of singlehood, well-meaning friends asked me when I'd get married again. I laughingly answered I wouldn't even think about that until somebody showed up with a dozen roses. Then I changed the subject.

That evening I mentally replayed the conversation—knowing I often veil the truth with my humor—and asked myself a tough question: Would I *really* be attracted to the first guy who handed me roses?

As I admitted that he would at least get my attention, I made an important decision: Plant my own garden.

The next morning, I was at our local gardening shop loading my trunk with 15 rose bushes and 12 bags of peat moss. For the next several months, I kept fresh roses throughout the house and quietly marveled at the freedom the bright blooms represented.

To Remarry or Not to Remarry Is an Individual Decision

Admittedly, I made a tough choice when I decided not to remarry, and—although it is not the choice every single mother will make—I feel it is the right one for me.

Why?

I genuinely believe my life would never have turned out to be this exciting if I had settled for what I wanted instead of what God wanted to give me. And I believe God wanted to give me more of Himself, not another husband.

I was also convinced the Lord was preparing me for another career, and I felt sure a second husband would just talk me into going back to the high school classroom. Besides, I'd seen too many problems in second marriages. The divorce rate nationwide is 50 percent for first marriages, 65 percent for second marriages.

I didn't want to be one of those statistics. So, recognizing that the mortality rate of second marriages is even higher than in first marriages, I determined to save myself from even getting into such a mess.

I was also afraid another husband might be mean to Jay and Holly, and that was something none of us needed. The old adage that "love is better the second time around" may or may not be true. But it's definitely more difficult, particularly for blended families.

Yet, having said all that, aren't I really hiding from life as some of my friends have accused me of doing? No, I've searched my heart, and I can honestly say I am not. Rather, I am simply drawing on the Lord's strength to rebuild my life. And He is doing that for me.

But Your Relatives and Friends Will Still Get into the Act

Women in my Southern sub-culture are expected to remarry, so I often tried to reason with aunts or cousins who made comments at every family gathering. To keep from saying what I was actually thinking—*that's none of your business!*—I'd often quote Proverbs 15:1 to myself: "A gentle answer turns away wrath, but a harsh word stirs up anger."

My friend Rose Keilhacker finally helped me break out of that anger trap when she said, "You're giving everyone too much credit when you think they *really* care about your decisions. They don't; they're too involved in their own problems."

I laughed in relief, decided that she, for the most part, was right and promptly stopped worrying over the comments about remarriage.

My dad could still irritate me, though.

In 1988, just after Thanksgiving, Jay, Holly and I were shopping with my parents, who had finally consented to visit us in New York. As Dad and I waited for the others to complete a purchase, I rested my hand on a display. He glanced at the rings still on my finger.

"It's time you took those wedding rings off. Get you one of those Kentucky coal barons."

Undoubtedly, he was concerned about how hard I was working, but I didn't hear that.

"These aren't wedding rings," I said. "They're my Isaiah 54:5 rings: 'For your Maker is your husband.' Besides, I'd never marry someone who's made money at the cost of another man's blood!"

Dad's "Humph" ended that discussion.

But the next year, Jay, Holly and I were visiting my folks in Michigan. Dad looked at my hand again.

"You still wearing those rings? When you gonna take them off?" he asked.

That time I pulled the rings off and put them into his hand. "Okay," I said gently, "now what difference has it made?"

He shook his head, undoubtedly wondering which ancestor to blame for my attitude problem.

Amazingly, as I stopped arguing against remarriage with him and the other relatives, everyone gradually found more interesting things to talk about.

So despite relatives' comments and those of friends, I made a conscious decision not to marry again. Remarriage might be a valid option for others, but I rejected it for myself. I would raise Jay and Holly to the best of my ability—alone.

When I could verbalize that much to one of my well-meaning friends, she said she admired the fact that I was *taking charge* of my life rather than merely *reacting* to everything. Then she leaned toward me. "But don't put God and His future for you in a little box."

I thought about that for several days and then prayed, "Lord, You know I want only what You want. But if I can have my druthers, I'd druther remain single. All I need are friends who will smile when I come into a room."

For Some Single Moms Remarriage Is an Option

But Make Haste Slowly; Loneliness Can Be a Trap

I'm amazed at the number of women who rush into and stay in abusive relationships out of loneliness. What an awful trap! And the entire time, they keep telling themselves things will get better. Yet they never do get better.

I learned the illogic of that kind of thinking years ago when I tried to take a shortcut home one beautiful autumn morning. I had driven Jay and Holly to school, and because it was such a nice day, I decided to leave the car in the lot and walk the three miles back home. All I had to do was stroll down the school drive to Joy Road, turn right onto Lilly and head home.

But I looked across the grassy field to my right. If I walked across it, I'd get onto Lilly Road that much quicker—with only wet shoes from the dewy grass.

So I started off through the field, glorying in the beautiful morning. Soon my shoes and socks were indeed wet. The grass was deeper than I had thought, but it surely wouldn't get any deeper, I told myself. I'd keep on.

After I went a few more feet, however, I realized the field had a gentle downhill slope to it. The grass that had looked only ankle deep from the parking lot was now up to my knees.

I paused, looking carefully at the several yards of grass I still had to wade through before I could be on the other side of the field. Well, it couldn't get any worse, I thought—my shoes, socks and slacks were already drenched.

In less than a dozen steps, however, the ground seemed

to disappear and the grass was over my head. I slogged through the ravine, feeling as though I was fighting my way through the jungle in some Class B movie.

But I'd gone too far now to go back. The worst was over. A few more steps, and I'd be at the edge of the field and on Lilly Road.

By now I was drenched from head to toe with the heavy dew. But, sure enough, as I plunged ahead, the grass was getting shorter again. It was at my waist, my knees and finally just over my shoes. I was free!

But my rejoicing was again short-lived. Just ahead was a deep, mud-filled gully. I stood there for several moments, looking at the muddy slope on the far side that would be impossible to climb up, even if I could safely get down this side.

In a moment of wild Tarzan fantasy, I even surveyed the large tree nearby, looking for a vine on which I could swing over to the other side. Nothing.

I looked back at the grassy field through which I had just come. I didn't want to claw my way through that again. Surely I could climb this tree someway and—no, they'd never find my body before spring.

I could do nothing now but turn around and go all the way back through that scary, wet grass. I finally arrived home, but in much worse shape than if I'd taken the long way in the first place.

But some good came out of that experience; now when I'm tempted to take the easy way out of a situation, I give it another long, hard look first. That invariably takes care of the temptation.

Make Sure You Remarry for the Right Reasons

Millie, a single mom rebounding from her loss, is like a lot of other single gals—she feels better about herself if she has a man by her side. For her, that's saying, "Hey, I must be doing something right. I got a man."

What she doesn't see is that he is rude to her, sarcastic and puts her down in front of her friends. She's one of those who's convinced she'll be a good influence on him and will eventually "turn him around."

Playing at Being Messiah. Actually Millie isn't alone. It isn't unusual for a woman—especially those of us who are doers—to try to fix other people's problems. Doers have to *do*. Not only do we keep trying to correct the mistakes in other people's lives but we want to fix *everything*.

That gotta-fix-it mentality's what makes us doers marvelous teachers, social workers, doctors and nurses. Give us a situation where we can correct a wrong and we'll try to run through a brick wall to do exactly that. That's such a common characteristic it even has a name: the Messiah Complex.

But it's those same compelling feelings that steer some women into making inappropriate choices in their mates. And we all know women like that—lonely, each looking for a husband and making the wrong choice, thinking this next

◆◆◆

No matter what the movies would have us believe, the world is filled with folks who have learned we *can* control those deep hormonal feelings and urgings with the same authority as we control anger.

◆◆◆

guy will surely be the one who will make her life better. *This time*, she tells herself, *everything will be great.*

She's lonely and wondering where the good men are. When she meets someone new, she eventually lets him into her bed in the name of "love" and then winds up feeling used—again.

Waiting for Prince Charming. In contrast to the would-be Messiah types who seek to rescue men from themselves, too many other single women are waiting to be rescued themselves, convinced they're not whole unless they're half of a pair. But if we're going to wait for someone else—that perfect man—to fulfill all our needs before we can be happy, we'll always be waiting for that mythical person to come along.

Why?

Because no other person can make us whole or complete within ourselves; only God through Christ can do that for us. The truth is that individual self-worth begins with our accepting what the Lord did for us on the Cross.

In the Meantime, While We're on Hold How Do We Handle Loneliness?

When I was in my early 20s, I thought gals twice my age were beyond being interested in physical relationships. Well, I'm that age now, and I've discovered that even a wrinkled face and a tired-looking body doesn't mean that the hormones are wrinkled and tired, too. Those little critters are ageless.

But no matter what the movies would have us believe, the world is filled with folks who have learned we *can* control those deep hormonal feelings and urgings with the same authority as we control anger. And if we're also wise, we'll discern the difference between the guy who's interested in a serious, ongoing relationship and the guy who's on the prowl for a one-night stand.

So Be Ye Careful and Be Ye Wise

In my files, I have an undated clipping from the *Reporter Dispatch* newspaper of Mount Kisco, New York, that reports:

> Men tend to misinterpret female friendliness as a sexual come-on, according to research by psychologist Frank Saal at Kansas State University. In one study, Saal had 200 students respond to a video of a female student asking for an extension on her paper. Women saw the exchange as simply friendly exchange. Saal concludes, "Men tend to over-sexualize what women say and do."

Because I'm naturally outgoing, this matter of how one's speech and actions are interpreted is an area that I, for one, have to watch. I'm fascinated by people and love talking to them, telling them my outlandish stories and laughing at theirs. And I'm so thrilled with the joy of this moment— one of the silver linings left over from School of Life 101— that my friendliness is often misinterpreted, as I discovered when the first guy who asked me out was married.

He was a known womanizer, and I was devastated by his

thinking I was *that* type. I tell myself, if anything like that happened *now*, I'd tell him exactly how appalled I was by his invitation. But back then, I merely said I didn't think that would be a good idea, closed the door to my empty classroom and sobbed at the thought of the situation into which I'd just been thrust.

That was the first, but it was not the last unwanted, uninvited proposition I received from a professional peer while both of us were on the job. I've always worked on free-lance projects, written scripts for videos, accepted special work with numerous organizations and worked with various photographers and artists. I treat everyone the same, and don't go looking for signs that someone is flirting with me.

Since I'm so outgoing, I didn't read the signs that a long-time friend and colleague in Michigan was starting to make a move.

He'd kidded me about being lonesome, and I wish I'd said right then, "We've just crossed into inappropriate territory. Let's change the subject, shall we?"

Instead, I thought he was being understanding and big brotherly. Stupid me! He'd even made little innuendos—going beyond the typical teasing—and was unkind to his wife in my presence.

Then one day while we were working on a project, we stopped for lunch. Little bells were going off in my head, but I thought I was safe. After all, this was a long-time friend. Besides, I assumed my weight was my protection; I was sure I wasn't going to have any of the come-on problems all those gorgeous, slim single moms had. Wrong!

We had other stops to make that day, so as we left the restaurant, I asked, "Where to now?"

He answered, "Well, we could always go back to your place and have a torrid love affair."

I was stunned but managed to stammer sternly, "I think I already have enough trouble in my life."

He laughed and changed the subject. But I wasn't hearing one thing he said. Instead, I rehashed what I *wish* I'd said—all the way from *I'm disappointed in you for making such a suggestion* to *You're scum.*

Yet I couldn't react the way I wanted to because I kept thinking that somehow the whole thing had to have been my fault or he wouldn't have said anything so outrageous. I now know better.

For since then, I've discovered that my introduction to the world of womanizers was mild. My friends tell me horror stories of husbands cooing into the phone, "My wife's visiting her mother. I bet you're lonely, too. Why don't I come over and we can talk."

Sadly, enough guys meet with enough success in these approaches that they think *all* single women can be won over sooner or later. The only way single women are going to get men to treat them with respect is to demand it with their own high standards.

Beware the Danger of Misunderstood Transference

We single women talk about those unsavory characters we've met, but what about those times when we're attracted not to the womanizer or the wolf on the prowl, but to someone wonderful—the pastor, a co-worker or a neighbor?

That occurrence is so common it even has a name: transference. All the energy and attention that had previously gone into the marriage has to go somewhere, so it's directed toward someone who is not an appropriate recipient.

Misunderstood transference can tempt lonely people into making inappropriate commitments or even into committing adultery. Too often we hear of a pastor who was counseling a distraught woman and then had an affair with her, further complicating her life while destroying his own marriage and ministry.

Unfortunately, that very thing happened with three of my dear friends. When I heard the news, I was personally devastated because previously each one had my utmost respect.

One had an ill wife and started meeting with a mutual friend to pray for her. That friend was a tired, under-appreciated young wife who looked forward to their prayer meetings. Soon they were no longer praying but still meeting, and their church rocked with the scandal.

Another woman worked on a church project with a

mutual friend. They'd been friends for years and hadn't *planned* for anything to happen, but it did. He lost his position in the church; she lost her husband's respect, and both would give anything for the affair not to have happened.

Another friend was the office "counselor," and he wanted to help a co-worker who was having problems with her ex-husband. It started with kind words, progressed to lunches and culminated into an affair that cost him church leadership and community respect.

Too bad they hadn't read Lois Mowday's excellent book, *The Snare: Avoiding Emotional and Sexual Entanglements,* (NavPress). One of the most important things she says is:

> If you have a special feeling for another person—and it does happen even with godly, married men and women—subdue it. Don't signal it to that other person. If you keep it to yourself and ask the Lord to help you deal with it, then you are the only one involved. But as soon as you signal to the other person, then he [or she] is involved. This ignites a fire in many people.[1]

Obviously, we don't dare try to fool ourselves by taking even those beginning steps that may lead to immorality.

And Don't Get Burned When Old Flames Rekindle

I'm glad I'd worked through those various issues that first year of my singlehood because one autumn morning I awakened with the thought *Set yourself apart. Be ye holy.*

The idea was so compelling that I even jotted it down with this note:

> I'm convinced it's a command, a warning against a coming temptation—not just a harmless little dinner dance either. I have on my desk a quotation from Billy Graham: "Be ready; the devil will set traps for you constantly." So help me follow your warning and your command, Lord. I *do* want only what you want.

It's a good thing I didn't know then that I was about to

enter three of the most tormenting years of my singlehood. All I knew was that I had just submitted to God's will and protection.

Just a few weeks later, an old boyfriend—I'll call him "Will"—came back into my life. He had contacted me shortly after my husband died, but I'd ignored his note. Now he wrote again, signing off with the simple "Friends do not forget."

I didn't answer that note either, but I was consumed by it for weeks. I was finding single parenting much more difficult than I'd ever imagined. *And I was lonely.*

More than once I paced the house after Jay and Holly were asleep, thankful Will and I had never been intimate to further complicate my emotions and glad that he was several states away.

And now Will was softly saying into the phone, "Let me back into your life."

I stammered, "But I'm not the same person you knew years ago. Besides, I've gained weight."

He chuckled. "You've gained a *lot* of weight. But that's never mattered to me. I've always thought you were terrific."

My thoughts bumped against each other. A man saying the extra pounds didn't matter? And how did he know what I looked like *now*? We hadn't talked since that Sunday afternoon 18 years earlier when he'd shaken hands with the one who would be my husband and told him to be good to me.

Adding to my emotional torment was Will's account of the divorce from his alcoholic wife and that he, too, had struggled with a drinking problem in the early years of his marriage.

And, to hear him tell it, I was the cause of all that. "I hit the bottle pretty bad after we broke up," he said into the phone.

We broke up? And all along, I'd been thinking *he* broke up with *me.* Obviously, we had been two dumb kids who needed to talk things through, yet had been without anybody to help us communicate.

Now that I'm on this side of the trauma, I'm shaking my head at all I put myself through back then. Those years were rough, not simply because I was trying to work through a widow's grief. But also, because I was having confused emotions over the way Will's life had turned out and over the guilt he was wrongly causing me to feel for his failures.

I knew I couldn't go back to undo past pain, and I certainly didn't want Jay and Holly dealing with trauma that had been on the scene long before they were born. I also didn't want to go through the rest of my life paying for an earlier mistake.

So there seemed nothing to do but just take my emotional lumps, lean on the Lord and trust Him to bring His good out of my pain. And that good, I felt, would be in His ultimately using my experience to encourage another confused single mother also trying to wade through the decision of whether or not she could reconstruct her life with an old boyfriend.

During that difficult period, I bought a wall hanging onto which I embroidered:

Lord, I have a problem—it's me.
Child, I have an answer—it's me.

Grammatically, the expression might not have been right, but theologically, it was perfect for me. In bright green and oranges, I embroidered flowers around the brown words and breathed a prayer with every stitch.

My tormenting thoughts didn't stop, however, so I threw myself into studying the Word and praying. I joined a Community Bible Study, even enjoying buying the complete works of *Josephus*, *Strong's Exhaustive Concordance of the Bible* and a *New International Bible*.

Then in further surrender, on March 19, 1984, I wrote in the front of my new Bible:

Lord, these new textbooks and Bible, which have just arrived, thrill me! How thankful I am to be able to study *Your* Word. I meant it, too, when I hugged this Bible to myself and asked You to so fill me with Yourself that everything else is burned away. I want to do only what You want.

When I wrote that, I was trusting Him to burn away

only my obsession with Will. For once we give something to the Lord, He doesn't leave it undone. But neither does He do just what we expect Him to when we've thrown ourselves totally into His care.

The burning away of people, of love of things, of need for familiar surroundings and of total control over my environment didn't come overnight. After all, those attitudes had taken me years to develop. But He was working in me, creating a new woman.

Meanwhile, the Lord was also putting things into gear on the East Coast for my eventual move out there. Out of my pain over the way Will's marriage had been destroyed by alcohol, I had begun working with Jim Broome, co-founder of the Detroit-based Alcoholics for Christ. I'd written an article, "What Makes Alcoholics Stop," that summarized many of the principles Jim taught.

Those 2,000 words opened the way for the offer of an editorial position with a Christian magazine. I promptly accepted.

So, remember, if you're juggling temptation and childhood emotional baggage along with your "impossible" situation, please hear me. Keep talking to the Lord about everything, hang in there and "Be ye holy" (1 Pet. 1:16, *KJV*).

When Ephesians 3:20 says, "Now to him who is able to do immeasurably more than all we ask or imagine, according to his power that is at work within us," it's true!

Maybe you won't be asked to accept a mid-life career change and move 800 miles away. But the Lord enjoys giving His children gifts, so who knows what adventures are just ahead for you?

But Remember That Women Also Can Misread Your Intentions

In the midst of all the craziness of praying through my obsession with Will and of getting ready for the future the Lord had for me, I was suddenly and sharply reminded of another hazard of being a single mother: being perceived by another woman as a threat to her marital happiness.

The wife of a colleague let me know in no uncertain terms that she didn't want me working on a writing project with her husband. She didn't like the way it looked. Actually, she really meant that she didn't like the way it looked *to her*.

Her words momentarily left me stunned and speechless. Limp with disbelief at their implications, I sank back into my chair and stared out the window to a beautiful lawn beyond. I may have appeared to be sitting calmly, but I was mentally clawing the air as her words catapulted me into the role of an imaginary "other woman" or would-be home-wrecker.

Any strength I had drained away, so that I couldn't even respond gracefully, "I'm sorry you feel that way" and then leave the room with whatever dignity I could muster.

I've never played the "merry widow," and I'm certainly

◆◆

If you're thinking about dating again, pray intensely and move cautiously. In college, "senior panic" was endemic among the unattached gals determined to get engaged by graduation. And now that we're older, a different kind of senior panic can set in.

◆◆

no predator. Yet I'm not angry with this concerned wife. For she did me a favor.

No more was I "Don Aldrich's widow" but "Sandra Picklesimer Aldrich—single woman."

And for that reminder, I'll always be grateful to her.

So, What About Dating Again?

I've been single again for more than nine years, but I still haven't starting dating. Not only don't I have time for that craziness just yet, but at my age, the only guys who whistle at me are in their 70s and 80s. And somehow, when they blow out their teeth along with the wolf whistle, any romantic effect is lost.

I confess I thought about dating as part of my research for this book, so I could report those tension-filled hours of wondering what to wear and what my teens' reactions would be when the doorbell rang. But I wisely decided that wasn't a good enough reason to put myself through the sweaty palms stage again.

My life is too full now to add one more item to my juggling act. Okay, okay, so I'll change my tune when that banjo-playing gypsy shows up!

Go Ahead and Date, but Don't Rush to Fill the Void

If you're thinking about dating again, pray intensely and move cautiously. In college, "senior panic" was endemic among the unattached gals determined to get engaged by graduation. And now that we're all older, a different kind of senior panic can set in.

When I worked on the grief counseling team of Dr. John Canine, a Detroit-area therapist, he was often asked when it is time to start dating again. He offered the "three Cs" as guidelines, as a personal measuring line: Companionship, Common Interests and Commitment.

People need one another, so dating fills the need of someone to talk to, to be with, to share with. But all too often folks jump from companionship to commitment, skipping the important step of common interest.

If the Lord has someone waiting for you, He most likely *won't* send him to ring your doorbell, hand you a dozen roses and say, "Hi, I'm from the Lord."

So, it's okay to let your friends know you're ready to date again. Everyone seems to have at least one "wonderful guy" for you on their Christmas list.

And who knows? He may *really* be as nice as they say.

Take the Initiative, but Be Selective and Sensible

You may have to initiate a few meetings, too. But bypass the local dances and secular singles clubs. If you want to meet a godly man, look in the places godly people gather. Start by taking part in your church spring clean-ups, joining the mission committee or teaching Sunday School.

But whatever you choose, do it because you're interested in it, not because you figure you'll land a man faster that way. Not only would the other way be dishonest, but you may be stuck doing something you hate for the rest of your life.

And if you're not sure that you're ready to plunge headlong into the dating scene, you can "test the waters" by talking to men in casual settings. It's amazing how much you can learn about their general philosophies just by asking a simple question in a Sunday School class.

I remember the morning someone used the phrase "normal family," and I innocently asked for a definition. The guy three seats over jumped into a tirade that ranged from blasting working mothers to condemning Christian counselors. I never got my definition, but I certainly had more than enough information about him.

Set Your Standards, but Then Stick Firmly to Them

Remember in the early '60s when our freshman home economics classes had a unit on dating? One of the first questions was "Should you kiss on a first date?" to get us to think *before* the date—and thereby set our limits.

Maybe we need to reapply some of that same freshman mentality to our present adult relationships. If you're thinking about dating, do you know what you want in a man? Or will just any warm, breathing creature do?

Perhaps my list of what *not* to look for in a man will help you compile your list:

- Never date a man who isn't serious about the Lord.
- Never date a man who doesn't like children, especially teens.
- Never date a man who makes fun of your cultural background, Southern or otherwise.
- Never date a man who is always borrowing money from you.
- Never date a man who says his boss or mother or first wife didn't understand him.
- Never date a man who says you'll never be as good a cook as his mama is.
- Never date a man who calls you by his dog's name.
- Never date a man who drinks—especially if he says he can "handle" his liquor.

- Never date a man who is rude to salespeople or restaurant workers.
- Never date a man who brags about the many "corners" he cut last year on his income taxes.

And my favorite:
- Never date a man who wears a belt buckle embossed with "Hello, Darlin'."

Okay, that's my list of what *not* to look for in a man. And since you know yourself better than I ever could, I'm sure you can draw up your own list of what you do look for in a man. So draw up your list, my friend, but give it some real heavy-duty thought and prayer first. And God bless you on your reentry into the dating scene.

If Dating Is Not for You, Sublimation Is

A recent movie shows a brother discovering his sister's battery-operated vibrator during his hunt for a flashlight. I was upset not only by the tackiness of the scene but at the implication that that's how single women handle their sexual needs.

But many do not. They have found other and better means of meeting those needs.

Before some friends decided I was hopeless, they asked if I was "seeing" anybody yet.

I knew what they were getting at, so I'd answer them with a quick "I don't have room either in my closets or my life for a man!"

But those who were closest to me would persist, might even clear their throats and then ask, "But what about your...er.. uh *needs*?"

I'd answer, "I try not to think about them" and promptly change the subject.

I wish I'd had then the quotation from the Colorado Springs Presbyterian pastor Edward K. Longabaugh to help me verbalize my goal: "Sometimes our needs need to take a back seat to the needs of others—not out of weakness but out of the strength Christ has given us."

Yes, Sublimation Really Works If You Redirect Your Thinking

So what *are* singles who chose to remain single supposed to do? Various authors have differing ideas, but most agree that the only activity that really works is *sublimation*. Rechanneling that sexual energy into our work, sports or other wholesome activities results in creative productivity.

In case you're thinking, *Oh, yeah, sure,* let me assure you from personal experience that it *is* possible to live a fulfilled life without that physical relationship.

How?

- By staying out of inappropriate situations.
- By not watching movies that will stir up all those old longings.
- By not reading inappropriate material.
- By staying out of the "Adult Only" corner of the video store. And
- By working hard and going to bed tired.

By pouring energy into other activities, we can smile at ourselves in the mirror and remain genuinely fulfilled.

And Yes, Sublimation Allows You to Enjoy the Company of Others

A few months into my singlehood, I awakened very early one Saturday and couldn't get back to sleep as I remembered other, long-ago Saturday mornings. Determined to think of other things, I asked myself a tough question: *What would you really like to do this summer?*

The most amazing thought bubbled up: *Visit an Old Order Amish family!* With my own farm background, I've long admired the Amish work habits and preservation of the old ways. And perhaps I envy them, too. But whatever my reasons, I'm glad I chose a new adventure instead of dwelling on what I was missing.

Within the next few weeks, through Indiana friends, we three were invited into the home of a large Amish family. What an amazing day!

All of the relatives gathered in the kitchen. The men were dressed in dark blue trousers and white shirts and took off their flat straw hats as they entered the house. The women wore dark blue or brown dresses and took off their large bonnets to reveal a smaller, white cap that covered their bound hair.

Even though I had dressed in a navy blue skirt and white blouse out of respect for their simple ways, I still felt over-dressed, especially as those beautiful, silent children stared at my watch and ring.

The clan patriarch politely asked about my work, and I told about what I did for a living, but I made sure I included details of my own Kentucky farm background, adding a couple of stories about some of our zany neighbors. How wonderful it was to hear the group laugh.

When our visit was over, and everyone was heading for their buggies in the barnyard, a sudden storm roared in. As the lightning flashed, the men lunged to calm the rearing horses while the women scooped up the frightened children. I watched the full-of-life scene with a growing sense of wonder.

Over the next few years, Amish families graciously welcomed the three of us into their homes. The high point on one visit came when the matriarch insisted we stay for the Sunday supper. Twenty-five of us were seated at one long table filled with hearty dishes that I remembered from my own farm days.

As I buttered a wheat muffin, I marveled at the long-ago Saturday morning sublimation that had resulted in this wonderful friendship. And none of that would have happened if I'd chosen the world's way of releasing tension.

What a Proposal!

You're wrong, if you feel the life-style I've chosen as a single mother means I'll never receive another proposal of marriage. For even though I haven't started dating yet, I've already received—and declined—a most interesting and unusual one.

I received this proposal when I was in Cairo, Egypt, several years ago with my church group. I was enjoying shopping with Kevin Johnson, the photographer with whom I worked, and with my pastor, Dr. Bartlett Hess.

We entered a jewelry shop, and Kevin and Dr. Hess proceeded to look for birthday gifts while I gratefully sat down on a bench in the shady part of the store.

A group of assistants stood nearby, observing me. I foolishly gave them my best Kentucky smile as a friendly American greeting and opened my notebook.

After a moment, the oldest one in the group walked over to me. He gestured toward Kevin. "Is he your man?"

What a strange question, I thought. "No," I answered.

He gestured toward Dr. Hess. "Is he your man?"

"No."

"Where *is* your man?"

Bewildered, I answered, "I'm a widow."

The man smiled, pulled his green shirt over his voluminous stomach and then thumped his chest. "I am allowed four wives," he said.

"That's nice," I replied, trying to be polite.

"Yes," he continued, "and for my *next* wife, I want an American wife. I want *you!*"

Quickly, I closed my notebook and stood up, having suddenly decided that I belonged to *both* Kevin and Dr. Hess. But my new suitor stood in my way.

As I sidestepped him, I squeaked, "Me? Why me?"

He smiled. "Because I want a wife who's pretty and *very* fat!"

Once More with Feeling

- Whether you ever remarry is your decision to make. But recognize that your friends and relatives will involve themselves whether you want them to or not.
- Our self-worth as single mothers begins with accepting what the Lord did for us on the Cross. If we're going to wait for someone else—that perfect man—to fulfill our needs before we can be happy, we'll always be waiting for that mythical person to come along.
- For you, remarriage may be a valid option. But don't let loneliness catapult you into an abusive relationship. If you do remarry, do so for the right reasons.
- Be aware that men tend to oversexualize what women say and do.
- Be aware of the danger of transference. All the energy and attention that had gone into the marriage has to go some-

where. But don't direct it toward someone who is not an appropriate recipient.

- Old friendships can hold new promise. But don't let yourself get burned when old flames rekindle.
- Remember that one of the hazards of being a single mother is being wrongly perceived by another woman as a threat to her own marital happiness.
- When you begin dating again, pray intensely, move cautiously and avoid "senior panic."
- And don't rush to fill the void. As you begin dating again, remember the "three Cs" of a good relationship: Companionship, Common Interests and Commitment.
- When entering the dating scene, you may choose to take the initiative, but remain selective and sensible. Set your standards and stick firmly to them.
- If remarriage is not for you, sublimation is. God can meet our needs, not out of weakness, but out of the strength Christ can give us. So choose the better way.
- Sublimation will work for you, if you redirect your thinking. Ask yourself what's *really* important to you. Then find ways to include those things in your schedule.
- Rechanneling sexual energy into work or other wholesome activities results in creative productivity and genuine fulfillment. And you can still enjoy the company and companionship of others.

Note

1. Lois Mowday, *The Snare: Avoiding Emotional and Sexual Entanglements* (Colorado Springs, CO: NavPress, 1988), p. 182.

THREE

GUILT, WHO NEEDS IT?

"If we confess our sins, he is faithful and just and will forgive us our sins and purify us from all unrighteousness."
1 JOHN 1:9

G uilt and I are old acquaintances. How come? Because, like you, I'm a single mother and I have to work.

Whenever I get the guilts about not being home for my children, I think about Nola Cole, a widow I met at a family reunion in Oil City, Kentucky. Her husband had been injured at 23 in the coal mines—strained his heart after pushing a loaded coal cart out of the way, she said—and died a couple of years later.

She had no choice but to go to work as a "hired girl" and turn her 2- and 4-year-old daughters over to her parents to raise. She saw them only once a month for several years.

Like Nola, most of us don't have a choice either. We have to work.

And with everything else we're handling, we don't need to lay extra guilt on ourselves. Others will do that for us quite readily. So let's just accept the fact that some things are the way they have to be and grab any extra moment for ourselves and our children that we can muster.

Guilt Imposed by Others

I went back to teaching when Jay was less than a year old. And one of the women with whom I worked in the church nursery was always saying in glee, "You're going to miss his first steps."

As Jay began to pull himself up and then work his way across a room by clutching the sofa and chairs, I was so tormented that the sitter and not I would witness his first-step milestone that I started to pray about it daily. Somewhere in the middle of my prayers, the thought came that even if I missed those first steps, there'd be plenty of other firsts to rejoice in.

Then late one afternoon, while I was preparing dinner, 13-month-old Jay worked his way around the kitchen by clutching the walls. Suddenly he giggled, let go of the wall and took three big steps right into my open arms.

The following Sunday at church, I had just put on my nursery apron when my co-worker stormed in. "I can't believe it!" she snarled. "We went to my cousin's wedding last night and left Becky with a sitter for the first time. And she took her first steps while we were gone."

Amazingly, I felt no glee that what she had wished on me had befallen her.

Guilt Generated by Stereotypes

I also remember one winter afternoon in New York when our company closed early because of an impending storm. I arrived home 30 minutes before Jay and Holly's school bus, so I quickly stirred up a batch of chocolate chip cookies.

I'll never forget the look of joy on my teens' faces when they opened the door and discovered I was there to greet them. They had barely shaken the snow off their coats when I exclaimed, "And I made cookies! I'm a mom again!"

That has become our family joke now. Obviously, I was trying to fit someone else's idea of what "good mothers" are supposed to do. I've since learned that, as single moms, we can't juggle our responsibilities if we let others heap guilt around our already stooped shoulders.

Guilt Exploited by Our Kids

Jay and Holly figured out rather quickly that I can handle a crisis but I can't handle guilt. Not only have they used that whenever it was to their advantage, but that's how we got Petey—the tiger cat that moved in with us five years ago.

For years, they had been asking for a pet, especially since they remembered our previous animals. At first, I patiently explained our schedule, saying it wouldn't be fair to an animal to be left alone so much.

They'd counter with the thought that a cat likes being left alone. I again said no.

They described the new litter of kittens in the neighborhood, adding that they'd be "put to sleep" if a home wasn't found soon. I remained unmoved.

Finally, Holly looked at me with her sorrowful eyes. "How come when we ask you for a kitty, you always say no. But the *first* time we asked Daddy, he said yes?!"

I knew I'd lost. "Go get your cat, Holly."

The Problem of Latchkey Kids

We already recognize that the guilt of the working mother is caused by the amount of time she necessarily must spend away from her children while earning their daily bread. By offering flex-time schedules to working moms, employers will greatly lessen our guilt by lessening the time we are away from our children. And the employer, at the same time, will benefit by gaining an employee with greatly improved morale.

I remember a TV show I saw as a youngster about a pioneer woman and her baby who were captured by Indians. The woman begged for the life of her little boy, saying she'd do whatever the warrior wanted if he'd let her son live. He killed the child anyway.

I left the room, muttering over the man's stupidity. Naturally, the rest of the program would consist of the trouble the woman would give her warrior-captor for depriving her of her son.

Even as a child, I understood the principle the warrior had missed: Let us women take care of what's important to us and we'll also take care of what's important to our men—male bosses included.

Ask for Flex Time When on the Job

When we moved to New York, my work schedule thrust Jay and Holly into the world of latchkey kids. I wasn't handling the trauma well at all, so I talked it over with my boss. He let me start earlier, so I could arrive home only an hour later than my children did. Not only did that greatly help my family situation, but the business actually got extra hours out of me since I often worked through lunch.

Like it or not, Christian women *are* working outside the home, and Christian organizations particularly should be setting the lead by offering flexible hours for those who want them. I'm not looking forward to standing before the Lord to give an account for my parenting. But I hope I get to ask that several bosses be made to stand there with me.

Check out Child Care Possibilities Locally

Most of us get tired enough juggling guilt; we don't need worry tossed in, too. Child care goes a long way toward alleviating a working mother's worry—particularly the worry of a mother with preschoolers—if the child care is good and if the cost fits the budget. Pray a lot and look hard around you at what is available in your area.

Here are a few suggestions worth checking on:
- Is there a church-operated child-care center near you or your place of work?
- Does your school have an after-school program?
- Do you have any older relatives in your vicinity who enjoy spoiling kids and getting paid for it?
- Is there another mother nearby who is staying home with her kids and who would be willing to look after

one—or two—more for, say, a monthly fee?
- Can the directors of senior citizens clubs and organizations—such as the local branch of the American Association of Retired Persons (AARP)—suggest responsible grandparents who could use the extra income and would enjoy the contact with youngsters?
- Are college students nearby who enjoy kids and can use some extra income?

Make the Kids Safe When They're Home Alone

You can probably think of additional ones, but here are a few suggestions of ways we can make sure our children are safe at home when we're not there:
- **Set up definite rules—including those for chores and visitors.** When Jay and Holly were younger, a major rule was that they couldn't have visitors if I wasn't home. Now that we're in Colorado, and they're 17 and 18, that rule is occasionally bent—but only if the visitor is of the same gender and if the other parent knows I'm not home.

  Krista Parkin, the teen across the street, came over to help Holly learn her lines for the church play while I was in California. Her mother was available had a problem arisen.
- **Make sure your children are secure and know who to call in an emergency.** Stress that they are never to open the door and are never to tell a stranger on the phone that they're alone.

  I always instructed Jay and Holly to say, "I'm sorry, but my mother can't come to the phone right now. If you'll leave a message, I'll have her call you back shortly."

  One of the men with whom I taught was angry with me one morning, saying he'd called, but Holly wouldn't let him talk to me.

  "You couldn't have been in the shower that long!" he snarled, guessing at the reason for Holly's deliberately vague explanation on the phone.

  "Oh, you're the one who wouldn't leave his name," I said. And then, though I was under no obligation to tell him, I explained, "I was grocery shopping."

"Well, she could have told me you weren't home."

"Why? She doesn't know you."

"Well, that's dumb."

The other mothers at the lunch table chimed in then, coming to my rescue and letting him know he was really out of line.

- **Talk to your children about their concerns.** Ask them what they hate the most about being home alone and work out ways to make that area less painful.

   For Jamie, it was coming into a dark house in the winter. His mother's simple investment in an electric timer took care of the problem.

- **Make sure your kids have your work phone number.** But insist they don't call you to referee their squabbles.

   Sharon, a recent single mom, remembers the tired mother in the fabric department who got a call right in the middle of cutting a length of material. Sharon could hear her pleading with first one son and then another, saying she'd help them settle it when she got home in a couple of hours.

   Sharon confesses that her first thought was *Why doesn't she stay home with her kids where she belongs?* It was easy for Sharon to be self-righteous: Her physician husband paid her bills; their children were cared for a few hours each day by a housekeeper.

   When her husband left her for his nurse, Sharon's world came tumbling in. Eventually, she even had to take a job outside the home. Then she remembered the fabric worker with a new understanding.

The Difficulty of Long, Hot Summers

If at First, You Don't Succeed—

Summertime—and the worry is heavy. Yes, summer is an especially tough time for us single moms. Jay and Holly were 14 and 13 the summer after we moved to New York. I sent them back to our summer mobile home by beautiful Lake Michigan and arranged for various relatives to stay during the week. I flew or drove back and forth several times during those 10 weeks, further wearing myself out.

The venture was doomed from the start. Several of the women in our lake neighborhood let me know I was robbing my teens. One of the kindest comments was "I think it's terrible you won't be with your children."

At the end of the season, I sold the place—not only to free myself from the financial burden but also from trying to please 40 other mothers.

Try, Try Again

The following summer, I sent Jay and Holly to an inexpensive Christian camp in northern New York for four weeks. I was rather intrigued at the personality dynamics that went on while they were there. Both kids were given the same four-week sentence, but they handled it differently.

◆◆◆

All of us have situations we wish we'd handled differently....If you were wrong in some way, confess it to the Lord, ask forgiveness from anyone you've wronged—and then get on with your life.

◆◆◆

Holly was convinced from Day One she wouldn't survive those 28 days. She looked longingly toward home, and thought, *How can I get Mom to get me out of here?* The first postcard I received from her was addressed to "Four Weeks Aldrich." Her subtle humor delighted me, but I was determined she was going to stick it out.

She shrewdly decided next to give me lengthy accounts of the campers spraying their sleeping bags every night to keep the crawling bugs away. I let her come home then after a two-week sentencing: "The longest jail term ever, Mom!"

Meanwhile, Jay looked around and said, "Okay, I'm here for four weeks. What can I do to make it tolerable?"

After I made arrangements to rescue Holly from the crawling things, I told Jay he could come home the same time.

"No, I'm not going to wimp out," he said.

I stressed it was okay to come home.

"No, I don't want you thinking I'm a wimp like Holly."

"Jay, I won't!"

"Mom, I don't want to see it in your eyes. Just don't do this to me next year."

I didn't.

And Again and Again

The next year, they spent time with relatives back in the Midwest.

Those early teens years are especially troublesome because our children aren't young enough to have a sitter, but not old enough to hold a job. I confess, I'm glad to be past that stage.

◆◆

Guilt can keep us trapped and defeated. And the Enemy...knows we can't do the Lord's work as long as we concentrate on our failings instead of on the Lord's power to release us from the guilt of failing.

◆◆

But if you're still there, pray a lot, talk to other single moms, look into church camps and—most importantly—talk over the situation with trusted relatives, dear friends and your youngsters. These days of summer don't have to sabotage your parenting.

The Importance of Getting on with Life

All of us have situations we wish we'd handled differently. We can't undo those times, but we can learn from them. If you were wrong in some way, confess it to the Lord, ask forgiveness from anyone you've wronged—and then get on with your life.

Let God

I know that little formula sounds easy to follow, but it is

not. We all know it takes some effort. Many people struggle with this concept of letting go and getting on with life, simply because they refuse to accept God's forgiveness for themselves.

I began this chapter by quoting 1 John 1:9: "If we confess our sins, he is faithful and just and will forgive us our sins and purify us from all unrighteousness." So if our almighty, perfect heavenly Father wants to set us free, how can we refuse to accept such freedom? It's ours for the taking.

Guilt can keep us trapped and defeated. And the Enemy loves to have us beat ourselves emotionally. The devil knows we can't do the Lord's work as long as we concentrate on our failings instead of on the Lord's power to release us from the guilt of failing.

Let Go

I've worked on a professional grief counseling team, but when it comes to dealing with guilt, my mother offers the best advice: "It's like plowing new ground. You can get hung up on a stump root and keep worrying at it all day. Or you can pick up your plow and go on."

I don't know about you, but I'm ready to go on!

Once More with Feeling

- We're already handling enough without the extra burden of guilt. Let's make a deliberate effort to accept our situation as the way it is and, at least for now, the way it has to be.
- Don't buy it when others try to heap undeserved guilt upon you and don't exhaust yourself trying to live up to someone else's idea of a "good mother."
- Remember, if our youngsters find us susceptible, they will work the guilt angle all they can.
- Flexible working hours will reduce the time we are away from our children while on the job. But it's up to each of us to tell our bosses when we need flex-time work schedules.
- Don't forget to explore child care possibilities that exist in your community, particularly if your kids are preschoolers.
- Set up definite house rules concerning chores and visitors during the times you are at work.

- If your children get home before you do, make sure they are secure and know whom to call in an emergency.
- Summer is an especially tough time for us single moms whose kids are too old for sitters and too young to hold jobs or to remain unsupervised. So start your praying and creative investigations early for how your kids will spend those long, hot summers.
- We can't change the past, but we can learn from it. Confess past wrongs, accept God's forgiveness and then let go of them.
- When we concentrate on our failings instead of the Lord's power and grace to free us from the guilt of failing, we're playing right into the Enemy's hands. Accept God's freedom from the trap of guilt and get on with your life.

FOUR

KEEP 'EM TALKING
AND KEEP LISTENING

"Rejoice with those who rejoice;
mourn with those who mourn."

ROMANS 12:15

R ain had fallen for several days on President Thomas Jefferson and his party as they traveled cross-country on horseback. In their journeying, they reached the river they were to cross and found that the rain-swollen waters had swept away their only bridge.

The president and his entourage meandered up and down the riverbank for a while until they discovered a place where their horses could safely take them across. Nearby, a man sat hunched under a tree. He stood up as he saw the group approach.

Then he spoke to President Jefferson. "Please, sir, will you carry me across the river with you?"

President Jefferson nodded and helped the man swing up behind him. When they arrived safely on the far bank, the man jumped down and offered his thanks.

One of Jefferson's escorts turned to the now-dismounted rider and challenged him. "How is it you dared to ask to ride behind the president?"

The man blanched, looked into the kind face of his bene-factor, then faced his questioner. "I didn't know I was speaking to the president," he said. "It's just that I saw *no* in your faces and *yes* in his."[1]

Kids Will Communicate When We Moms Are Approachable

That's what communication with our children is all about—making sure they see *yes* in our faces and that they know we *are* approachable. And to be approachable is a rule I try to follow as I single-parent my two teens. To do that, I endeavor to create a nonjudgmental atmosphere where they can safely say what's on their minds.

We all know the things that say *no* to teens: put-downs, sarcasm, orders, "you should" statements and impatience that cuts them off in midsentence.

But what about those yeses?

We'll get to those. But first let's look at what makes for approachability.

Be Lavish with Praise

True, sometimes we have to say no. But don't be unnecessarily negative or overly critical. Kids aren't going to listen to what we're saying if our facial expressions as well as our words announce our disapproval of everything they do. Most kids really do want to do it right.

When I interviewed West Coast counselor Jean Lush, she said that when she worked with her father she felt as though she could conquer the world. He told funny stories, offered lavish praise and made his four children feel as though they were the greatest in the world. Her mother, however, was frustrated by their fumbling efforts and often compared them to their Aunt Ida, the family misfit.

Guess which parent's requests were answered with enthusiasm?

Mrs. Lush also likes to remind single moms that many of the world's great leaders and scientists were raised only by their mothers.

A welcome thought!

Keep Them Talking

Just because children don't talk doesn't mean they aren't hurting. In fact, those may be the very ones who are carrying the greatest pain.

With Jay's busy schedule, I can't catch him for those eye-ball-to-eyeball talks Holly and I have, so I'm thankful for my long-standing rule that they both help me prepare dinner. Working together forces us to talk.

But we still can't expect to solve all of life's problems with one intense conversation. The human mind often has to mull over a thought, talk about it, put it aside and then talk about it again.

Chris said that after her divorce, her sons were relieved their father's abuse would stop, so they refused to talk at first. But gradually over the next two years, they needed to sort through it all again.

Dare to Ask

When Jay and Holly were toddlers, our favorite after-dinner activity was a walk around the block. I often peppered those times with my "What would you do if" questions.

When they were four and five, the questions were basic protection: "What would you do if you were playing in our front yard, and a man stopped and asked you to come over to his car?"

As they got older, the questions progressed to whatever they might be dealing with in school: "What would you do if your best friend forgot to study for the history test and asked you to keep your paper uncovered?"

One Sunday, when my kids were 11 and 12, I impulsively asked, "What do you wish I'd do differently?"

Holly shrugged a "nothing."

But Jay immediately had a suggestion. "I wish you liked science more."

I nodded. "I wish I did, too. But we both know that isn't going to happen anytime soon. Meanwhile, how 'bout if we get a membership at the Cranbrook Science Museum?"

That proved exactly the right thing to do. Every few weeks, we'd meander past the latest displays, while Jay explained what we were seeing. Occasionally, I even understood enough that I could ask a question.

I still don't get excited about molecules and atoms, but it was important to Jay that I give him an opportunity to explore his interest. I like to think those Sunday afternoons at Cranbrook helped him clarify what he wants to study in college.

Once Jay and Holly hit the teens, my questions got even more specific:

> "What would you do if you were at a party and someone offered you a joint?"

> "What would you do if your date said his/her parents were away for the weekend and suggested you go over there?"

By the way, they've never had to run from the stranger in the car, but they *have* been asked to cheat, been offered joints and been propositioned.

So far, they've handled all of the situations well. I know it was God's mercy and answered prayers that have gotten them safely this far, but the tired single mother in me likes to think some of that early game-playing with questions paid off.

But Don't Go Looking for Battles

At 17, Jay let his blond hair grow to his shoulders, and he couldn't be bothered with the current styles. His favorite casual outfit consisted of faded jeans and a Hawaiian shirt. When he had to attend formal school functions, he usually wore his Scottish kilt.

Just as he entered his "Scottish stage," he discovered an antique wood carving of a rugged clansman wrapped in a tartan. Hanging over one shoulder was a single, long braid.

As soon as Jay showed me the carving, I knew what he planned to do. "I don't care if you grow your hair to your knees," I said. "Just keep it clean."

He was active in the youth group and still attending the worship service, so I didn't think much more about it. But as the months wore on, I realized *I* was being judged for Jay's long hair.

Christian workers have enough spiritual battles without

accepting false ones, so I shrugged off the comments of questioning adults with, "Actually, if my hair was the color of Scottish gold, I'd grow it out, too."

But the most frustrating comments came from some Bible colleges that called to invite Jay to the campus for the day. As soon as Jay would tell them about the length of his hair, their first question to him *wasn't* "Do you want to know more about the Lord?" but "Are you willing to cut your hair?"

Isn't it a pity that we live in a world of outward appearances? We lose more youngsters that way—by trying to make them into clones of ourselves instead of helping them discover who they are in Jesus.

Anyway, Jay finally decided to attend a state university renowned for its chemistry department. Then, that decision made, he promptly cut his hair!

When I questioned him, he merely shrugged. "It's time," he said.

So, Mom, take heart and don't do battle over unimportant things. Battle drugs and alcohol—not length of hair, neatness of rooms or choice of music—unless it's obscene.

And say yes as often as possible; it gives more credibility to the times when you must say no.

Dr. Dobson tells about the waitress who told him of the ongoing battle she and her 12-year-old daughter were having about the youngster wanting to shave her legs. They'd had a miserable year because of that raging discussion, and the mother didn't know what to do.

What would the famous psychologist suggest?

Dr. Dobson looked at her and said, "Buy her a razor!"

And Do Get Their Response

Make sure your youngsters understand what you meant as well as what you said. Carol learned early that her son can't be bothered by the mundane and tunes her out when she's giving him instructions.

She now asks him to repeat what she has asked him to do. Otherwise, she found that she'd say, "You have a dentist appointment this afternoon. Come home right after school."

He'd answer, "Okay" without knowing what he'd agreed to.

Kids Will Communicate When We Moms Listen

Hear Them Out

Hearing them out means we must really listen to what our kids are trying to say to us. They need to know that we are listening.

Most of us are so intent on what we want to *say* that we don't listen. We're merely waiting our turn to speak. This characteristic is especially true when we're trying to impart our

◆◆◆

**One single mother told me the communication line
with her 16-year-old daughter opened the evening
she realized how her talks must have sounded to a teen.
The turning point came as she quietly said,
"Where you're going, I have been."**

◆◆◆

vast, hard-earned wisdom to our teens. *If only they'd listen,* we think, *they wouldn't suffer the same consequences.*

So, yes, we must do our share of the listening. Josh McDowell, in his "Why Wait?" seminars emphasizes that many teens are sexually promiscuous because they're trying to connect with someone. If they had people willing to listen to them, he says, they wouldn't be reaching out to others in inappropriate ways.

So set a good example. If you expect them to listen to you, you've got to listen to them.

Empathize with Them

And remember what worked for you when you were younger. Most of us learned through our mistakes. Why? Because, even when our parents tried to warn us, most of us thought we were being lectured. And we ended up learning a lot the hard way.

One single mother told me the communication line with her 16-year-old daughter opened the evening she realized how her talks must have sounded to a teen. The turning point came as she quietly said, "Where you're going, I have been."

One of my recurring themes—formerly as a teacher and now as a mother is: "These are *not* the best years of your life! It *will* get better—if you'll let it." Then I remind my listener that wrong choices about drugs, alcohol, friends and sexual activity will alter that bright future.

My students always seemed relieved when I'd assure them a brighter future awaited, but invariably someone would ask, "So why do our folks always say these are such great years?"

The obvious answer is that teens have choices. The older we get, the more limited our choices become. But in an emotional moment, adults often have trouble verbalizing that fact.

I've reached the stage in life where I truly understand that "Youth is wasted on the young." But I still wouldn't want to go through all those crises again—and I let my kiddos know it.

Share Their Concerns

Just before Jay's sixteenth birthday, he asked about the Vietnam War. I'd worked as a civilian secretary for a Reserve Officers' Training Corps (ROTC) unit in the late 1960s, so I answered his questions with my experiences. I told him about the hippie era and my own conservative denial of the reality of war until Clive, the handsome senior I remembered from my high school study hall, came home in a body bag.

But I still couldn't describe the craziness of that era or our soldiers not knowing who the enemy was. Finally, I decided to take him to see *Good Morning, Vietnam*. The movie was rated R, but I took a deep breath and escorted him. The scenes explained both the air of distrust that prevailed then and the Army's own way of handling things with far greater impact than I ever could have.

Later, over soft drinks, I tried to answer his remaining

questions. When I mentioned that three of my classmates and 16 of Garden City, Michigan's students had died in the war, he asked for specifics about them. I described Clive's farming ambitions and Bob's quickness on the football field.

Then I talked about Scott. He was two years behind me in high school. I remember the morning I first saw him as I came out of the cafeteria. He stood near the atrium with a shaft of sunlight falling on him, looking first at his schedule and then down the hallway in bewilderment.

I directed him toward the proper hallway and went on my way—never to think about it again until I heard about his death several years later. For weeks, I was tormented by the news. Even now I wonder if he'd stood in a patch of sun in the jungle, looking around in that same bewildered way with no one to direct him away from the snipers or land mines.

Even after our long talk, Jay still had questions. I could have introduced him to the war section of our local library, but since we were just a few hours from Washington, D.C., I decided the three of us would drive down to see the Vietnam Memorial.

How do I describe the sight of The Wall with the names of more than 56,000 young men and women who were killed trying to defend something they didn't understand?

Near the main sidewalk, two middle-age vets looked up names in the thick directory they carried.

Close by, a scoutmaster had a disinterested youngster by the lapels saying, "Some of them were my friends. Someday you'll understand what you've seen here."

Fathers held toddlers up to touch a name, whispering, "No, put your hand just a little higher. There! That's your grandpa."

I wept as I thought of that toddler's grandfather who had probably been in his early 20s when he had died, leaving behind a son who was little older than the child he now held up.

As we walked away from The Wall, Jay shyly looked at me. "Thanks, Mom," was all he said.

I put my arm around his shoulders. "No, honey, thank *you.*"

Take Their Problems Seriously

With all we're juggling emotionally, physically, spiritually, mentally and financially we can be tempted to shrug at what our children see as problems—whether it's uncooperative hair or having to eat lunch alone when a best friend is out sick.

Every time you dismiss present petty problems, you're closing the door of communication on future problems as well. Jenna's 11-year-old daughter chattered constantly, telling her every detail of the school day, including what her friends wore for gym class, what they ate for lunch and what they talked about in the halls.

After one particularly long day, Jenna didn't know if she could listen to one more account of who spilled chocolate

◆◆◆

**We can't assume that our teens hear our quiet
pronouncements....We must constantly say,
"Yes, I love you," and say it repeatedly through
a quick hug, a pat on the shoulder and...
by *listening* to them as well as talking and talking.**

◆◆◆

pudding on the cafeteria floor. But she determined that, if she still wanted her daughter to talk to her when she was dating at 16, she'd better listen to the pudding accounts *now*.

Finally, Jenna said, "Let's take turns, okay? You tell me everything that happened in gym class in 15 minutes, and then it's my turn to tell you—in 15 minutes—everything that happened at work today."

Not only did that give Jenna a chance to vent her own disappointment over not being invited to a briefing meeting, but it gave her daughter a glimpse into the hassles her mother was dealing with every day, too.

Get to Know Their Friends

Want your kids to tell you what's going on at school? Then ask whom they eat lunch with, who their teachers are and who's on their bus. Yes, that takes effort, but school takes up most of their day, and their peers take up most of their thoughts.

Melinda said she was terrified when she met some of her son's friends at a school play. She'd known her son didn't care about his wardrobe, but she wasn't expecting the wild hair, the army trench coats and the holey jeans his friends wore.

Melinda had the good sense not to demand that he get new friends; instead, she invited them all over for pizza and colas after the play. She's still not happy with the way they all dress, but at least she's confident they aren't a drug gang.

Recently she ran across a photo of herself as a high school student in the '70s and says the sight of her straight hair, white lipstick, miniskirt and go-go boots reminded her that teens do survive even wild fashions.

And Stay Friends with Your Own

Dr. James Dobson's advice about parenting teens is right on the mark: "Just get them through it."

I've found teens will test us constantly. And that's a tough ball for us to juggle with everything else. But that's just their way of asking, "Do you love me?"

And we can't assume that our teens hear our quiet pronouncements. As difficult as it is for us to do sometimes, we must constantly say, "Yes, I love you," and say it repeatedly through a quick hug, a pat on the shoulder every time we pass and—dare I say it again?—by *listening* to them as well as talking and talking.

Be Careful What You Say
When Talking About the Other Parent

Don't Belittle the Other Parent

Widows are often tempted to tell their children only the good qualities about their father. One of my friends did it too well—her son refused to play football, thinking he'd never be as good as his dad.

Divorced moms have to fight the other temptation: to

talk only about the undesirable qualities of the ex-spouse. But children of divorced parents often are struggling with guilt and loss of self-esteem, so it's important that we not add to their emotional struggles by belittling the other parent.

Diane handles this situation beautifully with her 15-year-old son. A few weeks ago, she introduced me to him. As we chatted, he said, "Some people think I look like my mother. But I don't think so, do you?"

Diane smiled. "No, you look like your dad."

Then she turned to me. "His dad is a fox! That's why I married him."

As her son smiled shyly, I thought about Diane's bitter divorce and marveled that she didn't transfer that pain onto her son with a sarcastic comment about his looks. Instead, her comments were an incredible gift of self-esteem.

And Don't Transfer Blame

Renee, to this day, is convinced she caused her parents' marriage to fail. She still remembers the evening, she timidly approached her crying mother with, "Why'd Daddy leave?"

In return, she heard only, "Everything was fine until you came along!"

If nothing else, let's determine to bite back those stinging comments and concentrate on getting through the days ahead. This restraint is especially important if the child spends weekends with the noncustodial parent.

When Clarie packed her two children's overnight bags for that first weekend with their dad, she literally put a piece of masking tape over her mouth to keep from saying all the bitter things she was thinking.

"My son and daughter were only two and four, so they thought it was a game and put tape on their mouths, too," she says. "We all looked pretty silly, but it helped me get through the day."

Most Important of All Pray with Your Children

One of my favorite childhood memories is of my Kentucky grandparents, Papa and Mama Farley, kneeling by their living room chairs each evening and praying aloud at the same time. I'd try to pray, too, but I was so intrigued by the thought of God sorting their voices that I'd never get through my own petitions.

I wonder what memories of prayer Jay and Holly will carry into their adulthood. I'd like it to be of the prayers and Scripture after dinner, but it will probably be the times of crisis when I began with, "Lord, you know I hate days like this."

Connie says her mother's prayers followed her all over southern California during the '60s hippie era.

"No matter where I was or what I was doing, I knew she was praying for me," Connie says. "The memory of her kneeling next to her bed with the Bible open just wouldn't leave me. Now that I'm raising my daughter alone, I'm trying to teach her to talk to God just as easily as she talks to me. And that means she has to see me doing it, too."

But what if praying with another person is new to you?

You take a deep breath for courage and tell your children that you'd like them to join you in talking to God together. Sometimes, though, you don't have time to have the family discussion first.

Vina had always felt awkward about praying aloud, too, but when her teen daughter threatened to move out, she remembered the comfort her friend's prayers gave her in a crisis. Impulsively, she wrapped her daughter in a bear hug and prayed aloud, "Lord, help me show this special little gal that I really do love her. Amen."

They hugged for a moment and then the daughter pulled back to look at her mother. "How come you've never prayed with me before?"

At Vina's stammered, "I guess I was afraid," the daughter hugged her again. Finally they were communicating on a level the teen could understand.

Once More with Feeling

- Your children will communicate with you when they see *yes* in your face and know that you *are* approachable.
- So stay positive and be free with praise as you encourage them to talk to you.

- Dare to ask questions, but don't go looking for battles.
- Say yes as often as possible; it gives more credibility to the times when you must say no.
- Get their reponse to be sure your youngsters understood what you meant as well as what you said.
- Youth may truly be wasted on the young, but their struggles are real. So really listen to what your kids are saying and let them know you empathize with them.
- Set a good example for your children. If you expect them to listen to you, you must listen to them.
- Share their concerns and take their problems seriously
- Stay friends with your kids and get to know their friends.
- Be careful what you say about their other parent. Don't belittle and don't transfer blame. He may be your ex-husband, but he's still their father.
- Most important of all, pray with your children. Not only are you wrapping them in God's protection and guidance, but you're making comforting memories.

Note

1. This story of President Thomas Jefferson was narrated in a sermon by Dr. John Stevens, senior minister of First Presbyterian Church, Colorado Springs, CO.

FIVE

GUIDING OUR TEENS THROUGH SEXUAL WATERS

"No temptation has seized you except what is common to man. And God is faithful; he will not let you be tempted beyond what you can bear. But when you are tempted, he will also provide a way out so that you can stand up under it."
1 CORINTHIANS 10:13

J ust before Holly's thirteenth birthday, I discovered that the oldest son of one of my friends was in prison for car theft. When I called to encourage the boy, he told me he had also fathered a child when he was only 15!

Argh! Jay and Holly dread my hearing about someone getting in trouble: they know then they have to hear the I'm-tough-for-a-reason lecture. This time was no different, but only Holly was home at the moment.

As I finished telling about the situation, I'd said that

when she started dating in three years, I'd have to meet each date before the big event and if I didn't like him, she wasn't going out with him.

She rolled her eyes and muttered that I'd forgotten what it was like to be a teen. I pounced on her words.

"No, Holly. I'm tough on you because I *do* remember."

We Can Get Through the Teen Years Intact

These times of sexual permissiveness and low moral standards are frightening for parents of teens. But we can't hide our heads in the sand and ignore the fact that so many young lives today are disrupted and even ruined by a few moments of passion.

◆◆

I've really tried to stress to my teens that their sexual feelings are normal and, in fact, God-given, but are to be controlled until marriage. And, I insist, those feelings *can* be controlled.

◆◆

In my first year of teaching in Michigan, two delightful 15-year-old students in my first-hour English class created a baby. In the years that followed, I'd have other girls crying at my desk after school, telling me they were pregnant.

One year, a sophomore told me, "But I don't think I'm *really* pregnant. We did it for just a couple of seconds."

Another year I remember a junior telling me she'd only "done it" one time. But one time was all it took.

The girls and I would talk, and I'd offer to go with them to tell their parents, but no one ever took me up on that offer. I wish I'd given more hugs along with my words of comfort, but after they'd leave, *I'd* cry.

Though I'm no longer the concerned teacher, I'm a mom who has to be careful that her memories of those students and her fears don't cloud her own children's dating. That's why I've made sure I've talked with my youngsters about their sexuality.

Of course, it's tough trying to keep our teens on the straight and narrow. And, I confess, that the best years for me were when Jay was 15 and Holly 14—because he couldn't drive and she couldn't date!

But we can get through this time in our lives if we'll keep our own standards high and keep talking to our teens about theirs.

But We Need to Answer the Unasked Questions

My own sex education consisted of my dear mother clutching at her blouse and reeling backwards in mortification when I asked embarrassing questions. She constantly cautioned me though that "boys are after only one thing."

That warning really worried me because I didn't know what it was they were after. I knew I didn't have any *money*.

Realizing how inadequate was my own sex education, I've really tried to stress to my teens that their sexual feelings are normal and, in fact, God-given, but are to be controlled until marriage. And, I insist, those feelings *can* be controlled.

When adults say, "Be careful that your feelings don't run away with you," they're conveying the idea that sexual feelings are so strong they can overrule judgment. That's an incorrect message to give.

Sexual feelings don't have to be acted on any more than feelings of anger. And I've tried to stress that point to Jay and Holly both in our discussions and in visible reminders. Just about the time they hit puberty, I put a 3″ x 5″ card on their desks with this message: "You may not be able to control your feelings, but you *can* control your actions."

What Is Going on in His Mind?

One area that single mothers are often reluctant to discuss with their sons is masturbation. One thing that helped me to prepare for that discussion was Father's Night for the dads of the sixth-grade boys at Jay's school in Michigan. I'd been single for two years, so *I* attended, sitting in the midst of all those fathers who were trying to ignore a lone woman.

The Statistic

The counselor, Gary Batherson, talked about puberty and

gave me helpful insight—including the statistic that 98 percent of all teen boys masturbate and the other 2 percent lie about it. Maybe those in that 2 percent really do believe it will grow hair on their palms.

Charlie Shedd, in his book from the late 1960s, *The Stork Is Dead*, encouraged parents to consider masturbation as a gift from God—a way to release the tension. Those of us helping with the youth group had used the book for group discussion, and that particular chapter got us in trouble with many parents.

The Controversy

Just a few years ago, on our way back to visit relatives in Michigan, I told Jay and Holly about those years of working with the senior high youth group and the problem we'd had over that chapter. I quoted Gary Batherson's humorous statistics about the number of males who masturbate, and added the comments from those long-ago frantic parents that ranged from "Jesus wouldn't have done that!" to "I'm pulling my child out of youth group!"

Then I ended with this thought: "I agree with Charlie Shedd. If occasional masturbation works as a release valve and keeps a young person out of sinful dating situations, then I think it's okay. It's far better to rechannel that energy into sports or work, but I've never been a teen boy, so things are undoubtedly more intense for them than I can know. The real problem comes with what's going on in the mind during those few moments."

With the miles rolling under our wheels, I told them about the summer of 1971 when I organized a drama class for teens at the now-defunct psychiatric hospital in Eloise, Michigan. "One young man—a freshman in college—was there because his masturbation habit had taken over his entire life."

Jay chuckled. "See? They're right when they say it makes you insane."

I laughed at his attempt to lighten the moment, then said, "Actually, he was overwhelmed by stress and had misinterpreted the source as sexual. He masturbated 10-12 times a day. Finally his roommates convinced him he had to talk to the college psychiatrist. He wound up in the hospital so he could get the help he needed."

Then I realized the story, meant just as an interesting aside, wasn't supporting my original premise that normal masturbation is, well, normal. I commented that if they had any questions in the future I'd be happy to discuss it further.

The Problem

Jay turned toward me. "How'd you answer those parents? *Do* you think Jesus masturbated?"

Sometimes my brain actually hurts as I try to sort through their questions.

"Well, Jay, the Bible says in Hebrews 4:15 that He was tempted just as we are, but didn't sin," I said. "So to answer that, we have to decide first of all whether or not masturbation is a sin.

"The problem, of course, is what goes on in the mind during the act. I'm convinced Jesus kept a pure thought life so, to answer your question, I guess He didn't. Kind of contradicts what I said earlier, huh?"

As Jay nodded in his forgiving way, Holly asked about the other students in the class that summer. I was only too happy to stroll down a different part of memory lane as the car rolled toward Michigan.

Stress the Goal of No Regrets Later

Some years ago I was the speaker at a college spiritual retreat. And that weekend proved to be an eye-opener for me; I hadn't expected to hear so many confessions from Christian young people.

On the second night we were there, one of the girls sat on a bunk and sobbed her story to me, saying, "I want to go back to the way I was."

More recently one young woman sobbed to me that her boyfriend had broken up with her after their intimacy. His reason? He was disappointed that *she* hadn't been stronger.

My friend Rose Keilhacker is often called on to give talks to youth groups in southern California. Once she was speaking at a church in Alta Loma and hitting hard the point that the teens were to make good choices now so they wouldn't have regrets later on.

Just at that moment, in one of those marvelous coincidences, the assistant pastor walked into the room and stood quietly in the back. Startled at seeing him, she stared at him for a moment and, in bewilderment, called him by name.

He looked just as stunned at seeing her. "Rosie?" he queried in surprise.

To her startled audience she said, "Back in Romulus, Michigan, more than 30 years ago, I dated your pastor. How would we have felt just now at seeing each other again if we had been intimate back then?"

Plan Ahead for the Dating Years

A few months after Holly's twelfth birthday and at the end of her sixth grade, she asked when she could start dating. Like my mother, I wanted to clutch my blouse and reel backwards. But instead, I calmly asked, "When do you think would be a good time to start?"

She thought for a moment, then said, "I think 16 is a good age."

I wasted no time. "That's a good idea, Holly. Why don't we write that down, along with a few other thoughts."

The Contract

So we dutifully drew up what would later be known as "The Contract." We sat at the dining room table in our Michigan home and discussed several situations. Then she carefully printed the following rules:

1. At fourteen and a half, the start of freshman year, a boy can come over to do homework.
2. At 15, a parent drives for group dates.
3. No "real" dates until 16. Curfew will be 11:00 or time agreed to by Mom and Holly.
4. No kissing until 16 for BIG PARTY of Holly's choice.
5. No going steady until college.
6. No getting engaged until Holly's college senior year.
7. No marriage until Holly's college degree is complete.
8. Rules may be added to this list.

Holly wrote the date—May 13, 1986—at the top of the paper and then we both signed it. I folded it and put it in a safe place. I'd just bought myself several years of peace—or so I thought.

The Resistance

Everything was going along just fine until we were living in New York and she turned 15. To hear her tell it, every girl in Fox Lane Middle School was going steady by the time she was in eighth grade. When she'd insist that she, too, be allowed to date, I'd calmly ask, "What does The Contract say, Holly?"

More than once she stomped out of the room, muttering, "I'm never signing anything again."

Somehow we got through the junior high years, but I dreaded the approach of her fifteenth birthday when she could group date. Sure enough, it wasn't long after her birthday that she and a young man from her class were the sweethearts of "A" lunch.

I had insisted upon meeting him before they could go bowling with the rest of their friends. He had the good sense to be nervous, but gave me details of where they were going, which parent would drive and when they'd return. I took a deep breath, knowing the next step was just around the corner.

The Pressure

In the months that followed, I could see from Holly's tension that she was being pressured. The young man had known about Holly's determination that she wouldn't kiss until after her sixteenth birthday since she wanted her big party. But he thought he could change her mind. And he was starting to display hostility toward me and The Contract, saying I had tricked Holly into signing something at 12 that had no relevance to the real world, and that I was being too strict with her.

The Discussion

One afternoon, I came home late with my briefcase packed with articles to be reworked by the next morning. But Holly was aggravated, so I ignored the work. For the next hour and a half we talked about present decisions affecting future relationships.

Holly informed me that the normal procedure in her school was for the guy to ask the girl out for their first date, and then they'd kiss. She insisted she had waited all those months and was tired of having that "dumb contract" forcing her to wait.

"Fine, Holly," I finally said. "If you want to kiss him, go ahead. But remember, the deal was that I'd pay for a Sweet Sixteen Party only if it *is* a Sweet Sixteen party. Life's full of decisions. You can't have everything."

The Decision

She chose the party and asked him not to pressure her anymore. I'd like to report that he was really impressed by her attitude and said he respected her for making such a decision. But alas, he broke up with her and started dating her best friend.

Still, just before her party, she received so much attention from several guys who knew about her rule that she panicked. One young man even sent her an incredible bouquet of flowers, hoping to be chosen as her escort that evening. But by then she was feeling special and chose not to pair off with one guy.

The Caution

The night after the flowers arrived, I had finally gone to bed about 11 o'clock. Holly was on the phone, so I called a "cut it short" to her and pulled the quilts around my shoulders. I fell into a deep sleep, yet I had the most disturbing dream that Holly was in her room, picking snakes up from the floor. She'd hold them up, examine them, let them writhe over her hands.

I woke up then, in a cold sweat, my heart pounding from the intensity of the dream. I looked down the hallway and could see a light from under her door even though it was after midnight.

I found her still on the phone. I motioned for her to sign off. Then I sat on the bed and asked why she was still up. She explained that her old boyfriend had called.

Suddenly my nightmare made sense. I told her about it,

and ended with, "Holly, be careful whom you date. Don't play with snakes."

The Resolution

She didn't date him again, and that phrase has now become one of our family codes.

Ask to Meet Her Dates

One day two of the guys in her crowd wanted to take Holly and her friend Krista bowling. I had hoped to put off "The Talk" a few more months, but there they were—handsome young wrestlers asking to take my beautiful daughter out.

The Talk

The Talk consists of Holly's would-be date having to answer a series of questions about his interests, previous residences and family background.

The latest young man was nervous and kept glancing toward the stairway, wondering when the girls would be ready.

I smiled. "It's okay. They'll be downstairs when this is over."

I gestured toward the window where we could see his blue car parked in front of the house. I uttered the typical challenge of a concerned parent: "That's a nice car. Obviously, you take good care of it. But what would you do if a stranger came to your door one evening and asked if he could borrow it, even adding that he'd take good care of it."

The lad smiled in sudden understanding. "I'd tell him I'd have to know him better."

I nodded. "Exactly. And you've shown up here, asking to take my daughter out for the evening. Her value is far more precious to me than your car to you.

"But even though we've met, I haven't really known anything about you before we began this talk. Right now you think this is ridiculous, but I guarantee that in about 22 years when a stranger comes to your door to borrow your daughter for the evening, you'll think of me and say, 'That ol' lady was right!'"

I let that thought sink in. Then I continued. "Another thing:

You two are just going out as friends, but I've lived long enough to know how quickly situations can change. So remember this, treat Holly the way you hope some other guy is treating your future wife."

His eyes widened at that. I knew I'd hit my target and won the round.

Word's gotten around the group. Now when a new guy hints he'd like to ask Holly out, the other guys warn him about The Talk. One junior told Holly he hopes I haven't changed my mind, then said, "I had to go through it; I want him to have to face your mom, too."

Of course, they tell one another what I have asked them, so I'm always having to vary my conversations.

◆◆

At this point in my teens' lives, I recognize that my prayers have more power than my talking does. So, believe me, I pray *a lot*.

◆◆

The Benefit

Only one young man refused to meet with me, so Holly told him not to call her again. "It's like my mom says, 'You don't have to like it; you just have to do it,'" she said.

She later confessed she was glad I had the rule because the guy was actually "kinda creepy" anyway. How I appreciated her saying that.

Recognize That Prayer Has More Power Than Talking

Those talks with the guys who are Holly's dates—as traumatic as they are for all of us—are almost easy compared with the conversations I have with Jay about his dating. Remember the days when the mothers had to teach their daughters to say no? Well, the modern mother is having to teach her *son* to say no. Fortunately, Jay presently has more involvement with calculus and chemistry than he does with girls—but not by choice, he says!

I confess, at times part of me longs for the day when Jay

and Holly are both adults, and I won't have to be so watch-ful. But my older friends tell me my job won't be over even then. "You just wait until your children turn into grandchil-dren," they say.

Argh!

But at this point in my teens' lives, I recognize that my prayers have more power than my talking does. So, believe me, I pray *a lot.*

I want to pretend my teens are above such temptations, but I taught high school long enough and have been a mother long enough to know better. We single moms may not get through this as well as we'd like, but by talking to our chil-dren—and the Lord—and being ever watchful, we increase our chances of raising our children to make sound moral choices.

And isn't that our goal?

Once More with Feeling

- We can get through this time in our lives if we keep our standards high and keep talking to our teens about theirs.
- Answer the unasked questions. Often children need you to anticipate and answer those questions they can't verbalize.
- Sexual feelings don't have to be acted on any more than feelings of anger. Actions can be controlled even when feelings cannot be.
- Counselors tell us that 98 percent of all teen boys mastur-bate and the other 2 percent lie about it.
- Stress to your teens the goal of living their lives now so they won't have regrets later.
- Plan ahead for the time when your teens will be dating. Know what you are going to say and do.
- Work out rules with your teens governing their dating and then write them down. Written contracts save untold has-sles.
- Meet your daughter's escort before the date begins. Get to know him before you entrust him with your daughter.
- Remember that prayer has more power than talking, so pray—a lot!

SIX

BATTLING THE BILLS AND WINNING THE WAR

"Better a little with the fear of the Lord than great wealth with turmoil. Better a meal of vegetables where there is love than a fattened calf with hatred."
PROVERBS 15:16-17

When Karen's husband died, she lost more than just his income; she lost the family wealth, too. Her husband was from a prominent family that indulged him, so he'd never had to learn to budget.

Even in college, he had his own checking account, which they replenished upon request. His parents didn't do him—nor his future wife—any favors by failing to teach their son fiscal responsibility.

Karen had been raised in a family that said you had to save money for a rainy day, even at great sacrifice. Her husband had refused to think about a savings account.

Once she said, "We've got to start saving money. I don't want to wind up as a bag lady."

He laughed. "You just don't get it, do you? I don't want anything to happen to my dad, but someday we're going to be left an enormous inheritance. We don't have to worry about a thing."

Inadvertently, Karen shivered. Why? Was it a premonition? "Honey, I don't know what's going to happen, but that's not how it's going to be."

He stood up then, furious. "Well, even if anything happened to me, you'd still get my portion as long as you didn't remarry."

She shook her head, somehow knowing it would be otherwise. And that's exactly the way it turned out.

Less than two years later, Karen's husband died suddenly, thrusting her into financial chaos.

Where's My Faith? You Ask

Some folks will be upset over my including this chapter in the book, saying that if my faith were sound, I wouldn't worry about paying bills. But it's always amazed me that the people who admonish single mothers not to worry about money are the very ones who don't have to worry themselves!

My faith is intact, thank you, and I truly do believe God provides for His children. However, I'm also a believer in the old saying, "God gives every bird its food, but He doesn't throw it into the nest!"

Other folks like to remind me that money is evil. Wrong. First Timothy 6:10 (*KJV*) says, "The *love* of money"—not money itself—"is the root of all evil."

Jesus paid for our sins on the Cross (see Col. 1:20; Phil. 2:5-8), but it's up to us to pay our bills. And because the Lord understands we have bills to pay, He wants us to talk over our finances with Him.

Pay God First

One area we need to take care of first is the tithe. Even though the tithe is based on Old Testament practice rather than New Testament command, I'm convinced supporting God's work is one of our responsibilities. For years, I've helped three missionary families in addition to giving to our local church.

Some pastors teach that we are to support our church

first with the full tithe and then support missionaries with gifts beyond the tithe. I remember, for instance, the late David Allen, a Detroit pastor, who said, "Support where you worship. After all, you don't dine at Bill Knapp's and then go next door and pay the bill at Howard Johnson's."

Good point. But talk over your giving with the Lord, and ask Him what He wants you to do with your tithe. If you're convinced you can't give a full monetary tithe right now, consider tithing your time or talent by teaching a Sunday School class or painting a mural for the nursery. The important thing is to give back to the Lord a portion of what He has given you.

A caution here though: However we decide to pay our tithe, we should do so out of a spirit of thankfulness rather than expecting God to pay us back "10 times over" or "a hundredfold"—as some preachers insist. We can never out-give God, of course, but neither does He *owe* us anything.

What We Need to Be

Be Resolute
Make Rules and Keep Them. The January 1, 1991 radio program of Christian financial advisor Larry Burkett offered four major resolutions we can readily adapt for our financial juggling:
- Use no credit cards,
- Reduce existing debt,
- Balance your checkbook each month to the penny, and
- Determine to conquer your biggest personal financial problem—whether it's overspending or impulse-buying.

To that list, I would add only these:
- Pray about every expense and allow the Lord to show you creative ways to solve your problem.
- Discard envy of everyone you think has an easier time. I know several married couples who are struggling to pay their bills, too.

Say No a Lot. Don't we wish we had a dollar for every

time we hear our kids say, "But I *need* a new pair of jeans!"?

I love buying clothes for the youngsters, so this is an area where I've really had to get tough with myself. One thing that helped me was to involve both teens in my check-writing sessions. In amazement, they watch the deposit decrease with each check written for house payment, utilities, groceries, car maintenance and numerous piddling expenses.

We single mothers can help our children set realistic limits by refusing to give in on the clothing allowance. It's amazing how our teens don't need quite so many clothes when they have to pay for all items past that set amount.

Some of my friends solve the problem by giving the entire budgeted clothing amount to the teen on each birthday and announcing that it has to last the entire year. But that won't work if you can't stand to watch your youngster spend the entire amount on a "perfect" outfit early in the year and then wear worn clothing those last couple of months before the new budget kicks in.

I don't have the money to give my kiddos their clothing allowance all at once. But even if I did, I'd probably give in, if they started looking pitiful. Thus, what works for me is to set an amount to spend on each teen for the year and then just say no a lot.

Think Others, Not Things. When we were in New York and getting bogged down again in longing for *things*, I'd pull rank (mothers *are* allowed to do that) and plan a day trip to New York City.

We'd catch the Saturday morning 10:03 train out of the Chappaqua station and ride for a spellbinding 55 minutes south. Jay and I marveled at the people representing all social levels at Grand Central Station, from the Wall Street broker types to the folks panhandling for spare change. But Holly felt as though I'd sentenced her to an unbearable day of dirt and noise. In the evening, when the three of us arrived home, it was always with a new appreciation for our clean comfortable home.

One early December Saturday, a fur-coated matron got on the train with us at Chappaqua and chirped for 45 minutes to her preteen daughter about their planned Christmas shopping at several expensive shops.

As our train pulled into the 125th Street station—the stop just before Grand Central in the heart of one of New York City's most tired areas—the woman looked out the window at the decrepit apartment buildings and exclaimed, "Ugh! Why don't they move out of here?"

Holly turned to me, stunned at the woman's insensitivity to economic conditions.

I nodded my head ever so slightly in acknowledgment, but the woman had made my point about materialism far better than I ever could have.

And Live Within Your Means. When we were a two-salaried family, we made purchases that were ridiculously

◆◆

Set aside the thought that, if we're faithful to God, He's going to give us everything we want. To insist that He will, denies the faith of countless Christians within the inner city, in my beloved Kentucky mountains and in Third World countries.

◆◆

unnecessary. I don't have to worry about that anymore, as we now live within our means.

To help keep my budget in line, I refuse to pay for adventures with a credit card. Even a little bit of debt can start us on a spiraling descent into financial disaster. Besides, debt is one sure way to have less than nothing!

We live in a society that equates money with success and blessing, so we American Christians often have a special problem in this area, especially since we want our children to fit in and have everything we didn't.

But, remember, God promised to supply our *needs* not our *wants*, so set aside the thought that if we're faithful to Him, He's going to give us everything we want. To insist that He will, denies the faith of countless Christians within the inner city, in my beloved Kentucky mountains and in Third World countries.

Be Courageous

You may occasionally have to use a little good ol' gumption, too.

When my Ethiopian friend, Marta, and her family arrived in the United States after escaping from the Marxists governing her country, she was convinced a house would help them rebuild their lives. But they had arrived in the States as refugees; she didn't have any money for the down payment.

After much time in prayer, she visited the local bank president. He impatiently asked her to state her case quickly.

Marta described the house she wanted, confessed she didn't have any money, but emphasized her hard work. And then she ran her fingers along the edge of his desk.

"I am here. I can fall this way," she said, and—to underscore her point—she gestured toward the solid desktop.

"Or I can fall this way," and she gestured toward the floor. "How I fall is up to you."

He stared at her for a long moment. Finally he called the loan officer into the room. "Take care of whatever this woman needs," was all he said.

Marta and her family had their home!

Be Creative

I want to remind you that we don't have to have megabucks to meet our bills. Sometimes you'll even find an article about creative ways to make extra money.

Turn Trash into Treasure. I once found a trash-to-treasure-type article that alerted me to the possibility that the junky old lamp in the back of my closet was a collector's item worth $100. Before I read the article, I'd planned to sell the old relic at our annual garage sale—probably with a $4 price tag!

Set Aside Now for Small Needs Later. In addition to the universal Junk Drawer, we have two special drawers that get us past little financial problems: the Change Drawer and the Gift Drawer.

Years ago, it seemed as though Jay and Holly always needed a dollar for something at school, so I started tossing loose change and an occasional spare bill into a small drawer every few days. More than once, the drawer's yield has provided enough quarters for half a tank of gasoline or even an impromptu trip to our favorite coffee shop.

The contents of the second drawer—the Gift Drawer—have gotten me through more than one embarrassing situation where I've needed a last-minute gift. Each time I find a bargain table containing such items as an Amish cookbook or pretty stationery, I buy them at the reduced prices and stash them away to await "emergencies."

Try a Do-it-yourself Christmas. Holidays can throw another heavy ball into the many a single mom is already juggling. During the approach of a recent Christmas, I found myself asking, *How are we going to handle presents?*

I learned long ago that the greatest gift we can give our children is a pleasant memory. Jay and Holly didn't remember the expensive toys and intense decorating that had been part of their earlier holidays—when we'd been a two-salaried family—but they did remember the first December when we were a family of three and had impulsively donned snow suits over our pajamas one midnight to make snow angels on the front lawn.

I thought of the coupon books they made when they were in elementary school. I still have the one Holly made for me when she was 7. In large, wobbly printing, she promised to help me with grocery shopping and dust the low parts of the tables. Maybe I'll redeem those coupons when I'm 90.

Well, it was time to go back to creative gifts. I still wanted and needed the four adults and 10 children of "The Lost and Found Gang" to come for Christmas Dinner, but we were going to have to rethink name-drawing. So three weeks before Christmas, and over one of my inexpensive pasta dinners, Arlyene, Kevin, Larry and I agreed that the only gifts we'd exchange within our group would be service or items we'd made.

Christmas was incredible! Our family part of the day started with our own early morning gift exchange in which Jay gave Holly tickets for math help, and Holly promised to do several loads of his wash. One of Jay's gifts to me was a sheet of coupons for eight long walks—a sacrifice for my non-walker! One of Holly's gifts was a free verse poem called "Parenting," in which she thanked me for being "a great person and mom."

Of course I cried when I read it. After all, many parents don't have things like that said about them until they're dead! Not having any money forced the kids to come up with creative solutions to their problem and with ideas I hope they'll carry over into their future.

A few hours later, our guests arrived for dinner, each bringing a special dish to create a bountiful table. When it was time to open gifts, we exchanged promises for help with errands, plates of cookies and delightful homemade gifts—such as avocado candle sticks. It was an incredible day—and all because we were determined not to let a lack of money spoil our fun.

Be Wise

Overwhelmingly across the country, fathers aren't paying the child support they promised. Many, if they can get away with it, avoid support payments altogether.

Others who pay grudgingly—and would rather not pay at all—work harder at getting their payments reduced than in meeting their rightful obligations. Just recently, for instance, my friend Allison received an official notice that her ex had applied for a reduction by half of his support payments.

Allison's financial struggles have certainly put my own grief into perspective. At least I don't have to hear ugly comments from an ex-husband about his "pouring money down a rat hole" to support the children he fathered. Nor do I need to cringe when the mailman delivers another letter from the Friend of the Court.

But I'll give that ol' gal credit. Allison had wisely thought ahead to have her divorce decree state that any doctor or dentist bills over $15 have to be shared by her ex-husband. To eliminate the hassle when such bills occur, she doesn't ask him to pay; she merely gives the reception-ist her ex-husband's address and says, "Get the rest from their dad."

And Be Realistic

Much as we may not like it, we have to be realistic and rec-ognize that—contrary to our rosy expectations, beautiful dreams and lovely fantasies—life isn't always fair.

Statistics report that after a divorce, the single mom's income is cut at least in half. And therein lies the divorced mom's greatest envy—if her husband had died, she wouldn't have the hassle of an ex, plus she'd have at least some money.

But widows don't necessarily inherit lots of money. I know more than a few whose husbands thought they'd live forever and had never "gotten around" to thinking about a will or to providing an insurance policy.

Because of my husband's forethought, I did receive a small settlement, but it didn't come close to what his salary would have been. In fact, I wish he'd left me even half of what people think he did.

Too, Don's dad changed his will to leave the bulk of his estate to his two surviving sons, telling them, "This family has always left the money to the children, not to the grand-children. Whatever Jay and Holly need, their mother will make sure they get."

I suppose I should accept that viewpoint as a compli-ment, but it hurt to think my children were being by-passed because I'm a hard worker. And, at first, I griped to the Lord about this injustice.

Then one sunny afternoon as I waited in the school park-ing lot to pick up Jay and Holly, I read Hebrews 6:10. "God is not unjust; he will not forget your work and the love you have shown him as you have helped his people and continue to help them."

The words were so exactly what I needed that if an angel had tapped on the car window and given me a thumbs-up sign, I wouldn't have been surprised. I've thought of that assurance numerous times since when those "it's not fair" feelings slip in again.

Try Thinking Double

Consider Double Duty

At least four close friends of mine are working second jobs—often menial—to keep from losing their house in the face of company closings. And many of them also roll pennies and nickels from the kitchen change jar to buy gasoline, just as we do.

It's almost a given for single mothers to have a second job. Allison works a double nursing shift on those weekends when her ex-husband has the children. Laura bakes and decorates cakes after long days as a cashier. Chris, an elementary school teacher, gives piano lessons in the evening.

Consider Doubling Up

Some single moms have to make even greater adjustments: cutting living expenses by renting an apartment with another single mom. Ecclesiastes 4:9,10 supports that idea: "Two are better than one, because they have a good return for their work: If one falls down, his friend can help him up. But pity the man who falls and has no one to help him up!"

Of course, it can be tricky to find a landlord who will rent to two moms and their children. But I know two sisters in Michigan—with five children between them—who prayed, knocked on several doors and finally convinced an owner to rent to them on a trial basis. For the past five years, they've maintained the home so well that the owner has made other rentals available to single mothers.

One caution, though: No perfect relationships exist here on earth, so talk everything through with the other party before you enter into such an arrangement. *Don't assume anything!*

Save Now for Your Retirement

Magazine articles and financial books give us hearty advice about investments, but most of us can't follow those tips because we're scrambling to buy groceries. We keep hoping we can save money "next year," but next year never seems to come along. Meanwhile, we find ourselves getting farther and farther down the road to retirement age.

If your situation is like mine, you don't have the funds to make even simple investments right now. But hear me. You must put something away for your retirement—even if it's only a dollar a week—in an account you never touch.

I realize most banks require a minimum balance of a couple hundred dollars. But if you talk to an official, that rule can be bent for accounts that won't have withdrawals for several months. Besides, something about seeing an account swell encourages us to save even more.

And check out the pension savings plan at your work. For many of us that's the easiest way to save since the money is taken out before we see it.

You might also consider an evening at the library so you can scan books and magazines in the financial section while your kids browse. Before I had to figure out ways to pay my bills and plan for that not-so-distant retirement, I'd never realized that our local library subscribed to every financial magazine and shelved dozens of the latest budget books. Undoubtedly, yours does, too.

If you're like me, you're thinking, *I don't have time to read the paper. How on earth am I going to have time to read a financial magazine or even think about a budget? And my 2-year-old would never peacefully "browse."*

Well, if your children are younger, you may want to trade baby-sitting services for one quiet evening a month in the stacks. In any case, this is one ball you dare not drop. You and I will have plenty of time to read if we wind up as bag ladies sitting on a bench someplace.

Inventory Everything

Household Inventory

You probably have more than you think. We realized that fact when we moved to New York and my insurance agent insisted I give him a household inventory. I spent several hours listing *everything* in our home—even the number of neck scarves in my dresser and a head count of the dolls in

Holly's closet. When I finished, I was astonished at the items I had accumulated over the years.

Financial Inventory

That little exercise spurred me on to take a financial inventory as well. A financial inventory is little more than a list of your assets and debits. Translated, that merely means you know the money you have coming in and the amount going out each year.

Make an actual list of your income sources and amounts, savings, investments. Then list all of your debts—including the house and car. Just putting that down on paper will give you the same sense of control it gave me.

Provide for the Possibility of Your Death

I don't like thinking about it, but single mothers die, too. Just in case the unthinkable happened, who would raise your children? Probably your ex-husband, unless other arrangements are made. And who raises them if you're a widow?

Update Your Will

Answering questions like these make us realize why we single mothers need an updated will to provide for our children—and to keep any ex-husbands from waltzing in and making off with our hard-earned estate.

As our circumstances have changed over the years, Jay and Holly have had various guardians. When we were in New York, Carl and Marilyn Amann—dear friends from our Michigan church—consented to that responsibility.

Carl and I had taught together for 13 years, and he and Marilyn have a proven track record with their six children. We had planned that if I died, Jay and Holly would return to Michigan to finish high school. But now that Jay has turned 18, he and Holly could remain here if they so chose.

List All Important Information

Keep a list of all important papers, addresses and other such goodies where your family can find them, if necessary. Give a copy to your lawyer, as well.

Do you have a pension? List that address as well. Some companies offer survivor benefits in addition to regular payments.

My few pages begin with information needed in the event of my death or incapacity. Then I've listed my close relatives' names and addresses, my lawyer's name and address and general funeral arrangements.

I also list the insurance policies for my car, our home and my life. Next, I've listed my mortgage holder and number, as well as the account numbers for my checking and saving accounts.

I have to fly every month now for my job. But I don't waste energy worrying about the chaos that would result if I died.

If you are horrified by what I've just said and are thinking, *That's morbid,* look at it this way: Being prepared for sudden eventualities is like owning an umbrella. You seldom need it, unless you didn't plan on needing it.

Involve the Kids

Children need to be in charge of their own money, so I provide Jay and Holly with a small allowance. In turn, they're expected to clear the table and load the dishwasher on alternate days, do light housecleaning and keep their own rooms neat. I accept their differing definitions of "neat."

In addition, I have a long list of extra jobs—sweeping out the garage, shoveling the snow, cleaning the closet—for which I'll pay extra. And, as a balance, I charge them when they miss the school bus, and I have to taxi them to class.

On some days I even warn them that my schedule is so tight, if I have to drive, the price will be $5. Boy, you ought to see those youngsters hurry out of their rooms then!

An important part of on-the-job training is knowing their varying abilities. Jay will step over piles of laundry and claim he never saw them. But give him a room to paint and the job will be done quickly and well, especially if he can have the radio tuned to his station.

Holly, on the other hand, can't tolerate a mess. She's constantly picking up things that even I leave lying about.

And when she cooks, she cleans as she goes.

Maybe your children are opposites, too. If so, you've probably already learned you'll drive yourself goofy if you expect the same results from different personalities.

Keep Good Records for the IRS

If you're highly organized, you'll want to skip this section because my annual tax preparation methods give logical minds headaches. But they work for me.

Throughout the year, I toss all my receipts into the middle bureau drawer. Then long about January first, I start worrying about sorting them into several piles—missions and charity receipts, free-lance writing income and expenses, mortgage interest, professional expenses and so on.

When I'm tired of dreading the chore, I finally declare a particular evening as "tax night" and rope my kids into helping me sort everything into stacks that cover the dining room table. (As they got older, Jay and Holly started anticipating the arrival of tax night and tried to have something else planned.)

Then, once everything is organized, it takes another evening to total everything and get it sent off to my longtime friend Tim Yoe, a Plymouth, Michigan, accountant. He's also led me—over the telephone—through two major moves.

Once I apologized for bothering him so much.

He answered quickly: "No, I *want* you to call me first. Think of it this way: If you make a big mistake, I'm going to have to spend even more time getting you straightened out than if I had some input to begin with. So let me help you now."

I hope you have that type of friend in your life, too. But if you don't, you might want to pick up Judith Brile's *Money Guide for Christian Women* (Regal Books, 1991) or Ron Blue's *The Debt Squeeze: How Your Family Can Become Financially Free* (Focus on the Family, 1989).

We *don't* have to wring our hands in agonizing indecision.

Remember, God Works in Mysterious Ways

Even with carefully thought-out plans and much prayer, life's circumstances don't always go the way we want them to.

Crisis

Shortly after we settled into Colorado Springs in August 1990, I learned that the buyer for my New York condo—overlooking a parking lot—had listed the assets she *hoped* to have by closing rather than what she actually had. The deal had fallen through.

Suddenly, I was the not-so-proud owner of two mortgages. Meanwhile, war was looming in the Persian Gulf, causing the East Coast housing market to fall. The first job I ever had was for 35 cents an hour, so I know the penny-by-penny value of a dollar. And I was terrified at the amount I

◆◆

The more I read the Word, the more I was...reminded of two things: (1) that God had promised His children trouble, and (2) that he would always be with them in the trouble.

◆◆

would lose if I were forced to forfeit my down payment on the condo. Argh!

Questions

I spun into almost two months of rereading the Scriptures that I felt had led me to move West. I fought the fear that I'd somehow missed God's direction and often had to shake myself mentally and remind myself that my motivation for the rapid move was to get Jay and Holly settled in Colorado before their first day of school.

The more I read the Word, the more I was reassured that God had opened the doors for the move, and I was reminded of two things: (1) that God had promised His children trouble, and (2) that He would always be with them in the trouble.

I'd made my decision based on the information I'd had at the time, and no amount of hindsight was going to change the way things had turned out. All I could do now was give the situation to the Lord, trust Him to bring His good out of it and stop listening to long-distance "friends" who said maybe I wasn't supposed to have moved since the New York sale had fallen through. (Why do people do that to us?)

Surrender

I fretted and prayed for weeks. Then I reached the end of my emotional rope: One morning on my walk, I said aloud to the Lord, "Okay, I'm done with it. Do what You want."

Wouldn't it be wonderful to report He sold my place that very afternoon? Believe me, I wish it had happened. But instead, my declaration forced me to stop begging for an immediate sale and to name those things for which I could be thankful:

> Thank You, Father, for this new job.
> Thank You for this incredible sky.
> Thank You for the sight of snow-covered Pikes Peak.
> Thank You for the good health that allows me to take this walk.
> Thank You Jay's not on drugs.
> Thank You Holly's not pregnant.

The next morning I randomly thumbed through my Bible, not sure what I was looking for. Suddenly I stopped at Judges 20—the account of the Israelites asking the Lord if they were to fight the Benjamites. Twice He told them to fight. And twice they were soundly defeated—having lost 22,000 men the first day and 18,000 men the second day!

Trust

It wasn't until the third battle that He gave victory to the Israelites. Why had God wasted 40,000 men? At least in the book of Job, the reader knows that Job, a righteous man, suffered because of a conversation between Satan and God. But I found no such clue in the Judges 20 account. I was back to having to walk by blind faith that God *was* working even if I couldn't see the results.

That afternoon, a Monday, I pulled the last of my savings out to pay the bills—including both mortgages—bought groceries and thanked the Lord we still had $34 to get us through the next month. I was feeling calm. We could coast for four weeks.

Complications

Then Jay came home from school. "Oh, Mom, don't forget I have to pay for my chamber choir tux by this Wednesday. And I can't be in the choir without it."

I held my breath. "How much?"

"Seventy dollars." He was digging into a box of cheese snacks.

The kitchen chair squeaked as I sat down. "Well, Jay, this is going to be interesting to see how the Lord works this out."

Holly strolled in then, so I had them both sit with me.

I opened the checkbook, explained the situation and said, "You know the prayer that went into our move. But if I've somehow missed the Lord's voice, then we're going to face some rough times ahead until He chooses to take us through the problem. And if I haven't missed His voice then I guess He's just trying to teach me something."

Both kiddos stared at the checkbook for a long time.

Jay spoke first. "No, I think God's trying to teach Holly and me to depend on Him instead of on good ol' Mom."

I pondered that. Then said, "Maybe. But either way, we're starting an adventure. We're going to see God work in ways that never would have been possible without this mess. And you may discover the joys of soup beans and cornbread, but God won't let us go hungry. My Kentucky days are going to pay off!"

Jay shook his head at the mention of the beans. "That's carrying a good attitude too far, Mom."

I leaned forward as I said, "And I'm telling you we're going to be all right. You just watch what the Lord is going to do. If He chooses not to sell that goofy place, then He'll help us meet the payments somehow."

Prayer

I continued. "Remember the story of how England's George Müeller and the orphans he cared for sat at an *empty* table and thanked God for the food they were about to receive? And before they finished their prayer, a baker was at the door, saying he'd baked too many loaves of bread that morning, and could they use them? Or a milk wagon had broken down, and the driver didn't want to take the milk back to the dairy?

"Well, you just wait and see how the Lord takes care of your need for that $70."

Then we prayed, thanking the Lord for His future provision.

Provision

The next day's mail brought an unexpected utility bill—and a rebate check from Allied Van Lines for $254!

Right now you may be thinking, *So you didn't have money to cover the purchase of a tux. Big deal. We should all have such small problems.*

True, whether or not we bought that tuxedo was hardly a life-and-death matter. But as a mother, I recognized that having the tux made possible something of real importance to my son, and that fact made it important to me.

As a child of God, I truly believe that what is important to one of His children is also important to Him. And He demonstrated that truth by intervening and meeting a particular need which—though of no great consequence in itself—was a matter of real importance to a mother and son seeking His help at that time.

In the following weeks, we watched pennies like never before—and continued to tithe. And, gradually, as God met our needs, every bill was taken care of.

His Wonders to Perform

Oh say, just as I was in the final stages of proofreading these pages before they went to the printer, a young couple bought the condo! I couldn't afford to ride out the economical crisis, so I had to sell at a loss.

A New Understanding

But the Lord keeps letting me know He's in charge. I'm also seeing some of the reasons why I had to go through this difficulty. It's certainly given me a new understanding of the financial crises here in Colorado—and across the nation during this recession.

I started a Bible study group for professional women at 7:30 every Thursday morning. One woman asked for prayer, remarking that her husband's business had failed last year and that her temporary job was the only thing allowing them to keep their home. In the past, I would have prayed, but my prayers for her *now* have a greater depth.

I've also discovered joy in being stone-cold broke: No one bothers calling me with a sad story and a request for a loan now.

A Greater Good

So, the Lord always brings His good out of our problems—if we'll let Him. And He'll always provide for us, but sometimes we have to get a little creative.

If my brakes had gone out on the car while we had only the $34, I would have been in trouble since I'm too stubborn to ask even the church for help. I would have been more prone to barter services—offer to clean the repair office for several weeks or even provide child care for the mechanic's baby.

Occasionally, I'm asked if I'd go on welfare if I had to. That phrase "had to" is tough to define, so I usually mutter that I trust the Lord to keep meeting our needs. But if someone is desperate, and no help is available except welfare, then, by all means, I want her to keep feeding her children.

A Deeper Faith

My concern is for those who look first to the government for help instead of to the Lord. I've also seen what the welfare system has done to my beloved Kentucky, robbing many of the people of that wonderful, tough mountain ingenuity.

So let's try, as single moms, to be a little more faith-filled and creative than the rest of the world.

Once More with Feeling

- Money itself isn't evil. First Timothy 6:10 says, "the *love* of money is the root of all evil." The Lord understands we have bills to pay, and He wants us to talk over our finances with Him.

- The tithe is not an obligation but a privilege allowing us to have a part in God's work. We are to give as He prospers us, so remember to pay God first.
- Apply these four suggestions for gaining financial control: Use no credit cards, reduce existing debt, balance your checkbook each month and determine to conquer your biggest personal financial problem.
- Pray about every expense and allow the Lord to show you creative ways to solve your problem.
- Be both courageous and creative as you look for ways to stretch your budget.
- Dwell on Hebrews 6:10 rather than life's unfairness: "God is not unjust; he will not forget your work and the love you have shown him as you have helped his people and continue to help them."
- Retirement planning isn't an *option* for us, but a *must.*
- Don't be intimidated by words such as "budget" and "financial inventory." Those are ways to gain control over your financial life.
- Making a will and choosing guardians for your children are safeguards against your childrens' future.
- Children need to be in charge of a small amount of money. An allowance or opportunities to make extra money teach important lessons.
- Keep good records for the IRS.
- Though He may work in mysterious ways, His wonders to perform, know that God is always in control.

◆◆◆◆◆◆◆◆◆◆◆◆◆◆◆◆◆◆◆ SEVEN ◆◆◆◆◆◆◆◆◆◆◆◆◆◆◆◆◆◆◆

ANY HOUSEBOATS
FOR SALE OR RENT?

◆◆◆

*"Suppose one of you wants to build a
tower. Will [you] not first sit down and
estimate the cost to see if [you have]
enough money to complete it?"*
LUKE 14:28

'm one of those who never gets on a plane without
knowing where the emergency doors are. And when I
check into a hotel, I locate my floor's exit. Once I've determined my route of escape, then I go about my normal,
cheerful business.

Jay and Holly have watched me do that for years, so
when we were traveling together a few years ago, they insisted I stop thinking the worst. I assured them I was merely
being prepared "just in case." But I gave in to their insis-
tence, and that night in our hotel I didn't look for the stairs
nearest our room.

You know what happened next, of course. Yep, early the
next morning, the fire bell went off. For a startled moment, we
looked at one another, not believing what we were hearing.

But I was the adult, so with seeming calmness I announced, "It's okay. Let's just get out of here."

I opened the door, and we stepped out into a pitch black hallway. Not even the usual exit lights were visible.

"O Lord, help us," I implored.

Immediately, we heard a woman speaking with a heavy Spanish accent. "Is anyone on this floor?" she asked.

"Three of us," I answered.

"Come this way," she said. "Follow my voice."

With Jay and Holly hanging onto my arms, I felt along the wall as we quickly moved toward the woman. At last we could see her in her chambermaid uniform, standing near the fire door.

I thanked her, but she waved toward the door. "It's okay. But do hurry."

The fire was quickly contained, and we were able to return to our rooms to claim our luggage for checkout. But Jay and Holly have never again teased me about being prepared "just in case."

Avoid Surprises

Being prepared is just a part of my nature now. That approach to life and the fact that I don't like surprises—even happy surprises—causes me to put a lot of preparation and energy into making sure any major purchase I make is right for me and my family.

As a single mom, I have found that the two biggest headaches have been what to drive and where to live. And since I suspect these are probably problem areas for you, too, let s take a look at what is involved in buying a car and buying or renting a house, as the Lord and the budget permit.

What to Drive

Learn How to Do Simple Auto Maintenance

Before my husband's illness, my world was divided into neat little categories labeled "his job" and "my job." Taking care of the cars was definitely on the husband side of things, so I never thought about needing transmission fluid, changing the oil every 3,000 miles or pumping my own gasoline.

Pumping Gas. Then the day finally came when I had to get some gas. I knew it would be much cheaper if I pumped the gas myself instead of having an attendant do it. But, to me, the whole process seemed terribly complicated and dangerous.

What if I did something wrong? Would I blow up the whole city block?

I could already see the headlines:

Dumb Woman Driver Pumps Own Gas And Blows Up Town

Though I didn't know much about cars, I did know enough to realize that, without gasoline, I'd find myself stranded on the shoulder of I-94 real soon. Finally, after driving on empty for two days, I decided it was time to face The Mysterious Pump.

I pulled into a Meijer's Thrifty Acres gas station and got out to study The Pump. To my great surprise—and relief—I saw the directions written on the side. Whew! I'm not very mechanical, but I can read.

And what I read was basically a five-step process:

1. Unscrew the gas cap.
2. Take pump handle out of holder.
3. Turn pump switch to *on* position.
4. Insert nozzle into car's gas tank.
5. Squeeze.

When I looked up from reading the directions, a man who had just finished pumping gas into his own car was giving me a puzzled look. I tried to smile.

"I've never pumped gas before," I said. "In fact, I'd really appreciate it if you'd watch to make sure I don't blow up this end of town."

He laughed, thinking I was kidding, but he stood next to me, murmuring an encouraging "That's right. Good. You'll be a pro at this in no time."

Maintaining Fluid Levels. It seems funny now, but at the time all this learning how to pump gas was serious business. So serious, in fact, that I was determined to tackle other great mysteries in car maintenance *someday*.

That opportunity came sooner than I expected. One afternoon, I had just straightened up from putting the latest license plates on the car when our neighbor Bill Fife pulled into his drive. Seeing the pliers in my hand, he strolled over to see if I needed help. When I proudly explained what I had just accomplished, he nodded.

"That's great," he teased, "But I won't be impressed until I come home and see you working *under* the car."

I had my challenge. That evening, I invited my other special neighbors, Keith and Betty Thompson, over for coffee and forewarned them that I was going to ask how to maintain my car.

Keith's a natural teacher, so we stood in my driveway with the hood of my car open to a mysterious view of The Engine. And that night I had my first lesson in maintaining my old blue station wagon: keeping the levels up of the transmission fluid and power steering fluid.

I still have the 3" x 5" card on which I'd written:

> Transmission fluid—start car, keep engine running, open hood and stand on right side of engine. Measuring stick is black and located near the dashboard side of engine.
>
> To add power steering fluid—stand in front of opened hood (do *not* have engine running). Find a little blue-black cap with short measurer.

Changing the Oil. The next night, Keith changed my oil while I took notes. Those yellowed pages contain such practical information as:

> Watch—the drain plug is beneath the front left tire and is the funny button in the middle of the second-from-front bump. Put papers and pan down before releasing plug. Turn plug clockwise (move handle toward front). The oil is hot—be careful. Don't forget to put plug in *immediately* after draining.

The instructions about changing the oil filter include a quotation from Keith:

Don't rush—make sure you have all afternoon.

Next to that statement, I've written a note to myself:

Make sure *Keith* is home.

The first time I changed the oil by myself, not only did I make sure Keith was home, but I timed it so that Bill—the neighbor who had handed me the original challenge—would be pulling into his drive while I was under my car. He was duly impressed.

That little scene took place in the early 1980s, before the popularity of the 10-minute oil change pits. Now I take my

◆◆◆

An understanding of engines isn't inherently the preserve of the male mind. So whatever you do, don't panic when you look under the hood of your car.

◆◆◆

car to them and pay the few dollars every 3,000 miles. But I'm still proud that I *can* change my own oil if I want to or need to.

Avoiding Panic. An understanding of engines isn't inherently the preserve of the male mind. So whatever you do, don't panic when you look under the hood of your car. If I can figure out the workings of some of those strange shapes in there, you can, too.

The more you understand about your car, the less afraid of it you'll be and the less likely you'll be taken in by a not-so-honest mechanic. A good place to start learning is by reading the owner's manual that comes with the car—if you haven't already tossed it or lost it. I finally got around to reading the one that had been lying untouched in the glove compartment of my own car since Day One.

Also, many community colleges offer basic mainte-nance courses. It's worth a couple evenings of your time to learn about your car, so you'll no longer fear it.

Finding a Reputable Repair Shop. The best thing you can do to keep your car running smoothly for a long time is to have it maintained regularly. So ask your friends for recommendations of reputable repairmen. For myself, I depend on the service department of my make's local dealership.

Know What to Look for When Buying a Used Car

And why should you consider buying a used car? Because it costs less than a new one.

Yet, we've all heard it said that when you buy a used car you may be buying someone else's problems. Yes, that's why your reputable mechanic is going to be invaluable to you if you don't have a trusted friend to help you pick out another car.

So remember this rule, even if you remember no other: *Before you buy a used car, make sure the seller will agree to your having it checked out by your own mechanic.* That checkup may cost you any where from $20 to $40, but it will be worth it in the long run.

Where to Start. If you don't have a predetermined car manufacturer in mind and don't have the foggiest notion where to begin, just keep calm and do your homework. Sure, that's work, but you're used to hard work. After all, you're a single mom!

Here are some tips:

- **Take a trip to the library some evening after work and thumb through** *Consumer Reports* **to see which cars have the best safety and maintenance records.** If your kids are old enough, take them along with you to the library, and—while you bone up on cars—they can be enjoying the children's book section or the computer room, flipping through magazines or selecting their cache of books to take home.

  If your youngsters are too little to enjoy the library, get a friend to stay with them or hire a sitter for the evening. Even if a sitter's fee strains the budget a bit at the time, you'll find the money well invested because of what you'll eventually save with your newly acquired smarts in a wise car buy later.

- **Call your insurance agent for his recommendation on a car.** Your insurance can vary considerably with year, make and model, so you need to consider the cost of insurance protection before you start looking.
- **Start looking for a car within your own social group.** It's the best place to start, as a friend will usually tell you if something is wrong with a car he is hoping to sell you. Don't forget to check the bulletin boards at work, too.
- **Know how much you can afford to pay.** And once you've set that figure, don't allow yourself to be talked into spending "just a little bit more." Those multiplied "little bits" are what keep us all enslaved to debt. As a general rule, credit unions and banks usually will lend only 80 percent of a car's cost, so you'll need a cushion.

Christian financial advisor Larry Burkett says if we can't afford to save for a major purchase, then we can't afford the purchase. But while I agree with that statement in principle, I also know the reality of needing a car and not having the savings to cover it.

What to Ask. Jay and Holly occasionally go through stages of thinking they want a car, so they study the classifieds for days. Then they start making the calls. They even have a list of questions:

1. What's the general condition?
2. May I have my mechanic check it over?
3. Can the car pass the emissions test? That's an important question in our state because if it can't, we can't get license plates for it.
4. Would you recommend this as my first car? I've been pleased by the sellers who've warned them not to buy their car since that particular model had a lot of problems.

So far, Jay and Holly haven't found anything they can afford that meets all those criteria, so we're still a one-car family. But when they do finally get their car, it's going to be one they've worked hard for. And I'm sure they'll appreciate it much more.

How to Proceed. After you've done your homework, you can start visiting the car lots. Many magazine articles suggest you take a male friend along, but that's impossible for those of us who have moved away from our friends. As a rule, I've found most salesmen want to be helpful, so don't assume every used car salesman is out to cheat you.

If the salesman is rude—as one was to Allison with his "Tell you what, honey, why don't you have your husband come in and talk to me?"—politely tell him you're taking your business someplace else because of his rudeness and then leave. But scenes like that are rare, so don't walk in with a chip on your shoulder.

Whatever else you do, just don't buy the first thing you look at—if for no other reason than to satisfy your own future questions about what else might have been available. And, as you visit the various car lots, do carry a notebook to jot down important details: size of car, whether it's a 4- or 6-cylinder (the number of cylinders merely determines the power you'll have on the expressway), the general condition and the price.

Next, ask to see the "blue book" price on that car. If you belong to a credit union, give them a quick phone call and they'll be happy to supply that information. The "blue book" is published by the National Automobile Dealers Association and is properly called the *NADA Official Used Car Guide.*

It lists the average trade-in value, the retail price and the amount of credit you can expect to receive for it. But remember that their listing is made up of averages. How much you pay for your particular car will depend on the car's condition, supply-and-demand, the locale and the trade-in value of your present car—if you have one.

What to Look For. All I'd ever seen anyone do in the movies was kick the tires—a sure sign of an amateur. So, when the station wagon's engine went out, I talked to anybody who was interested in cars, asked questions and read the magazine articles. From all that, I developed a mental list of what I needed in a car: four doors, a big trunk and enough engine power to keep me safely on our Detroit expressway.

I also quizzed my neighbor Keith Thompson on the specifics of what to look for in a used car.

Here are some of the things I learned:

- **Check the car's exterior.** Look for dents, rust, discolored paint and welding ripples. Metal ripples or uneven paint are clues that the car has been in an accident. That's especially important to know if the frame was bent.

  And deep rust means the car is rusting from the inside out. That problem could mean a major repair will be due soon.

- **Check the interior.** Examine the controls—wipers, heat and air, turn signals, radio and all lights. And look under the mats and loose carpet for rust.

  Also look at the odometer to check the mileage. Then look at the gas pedal. If the pedal's well worn, but the odometer shows low mileage, that's a pretty good sign they've rolled back the mileage. Also, if the numbers don't line up evenly, someone has been messing with the odometer.

- **Look under the hood.** This is the scary part for me. Are the belts and hoses worn? Does the radiator show corrosion or rust around the cap? Is the battery corroded? Does it have worn cables?

- **Start the engine.** As the car idles, accelerate and listen for pings or knocks. That's a sign of potential engine problems. Keith talked about "valves" and "rings" in the same sentence as "knocks," but it all translated into "engine problems."

  Keith also said to let the car run for five minutes, then check under it for puddles. If they're greasy, you could have transmission problems.

- **Take the car for a drive.** It's called a "test drive," because you're supposed to be *testing* the brakes, steering and general handling.

- **Trust your instincts.** Listen for unusual noises when you shift, accelerate or brake. Don't ignore any pulling or jerking.

See? It's not so scary when you know what you're looking for.

Know What to Do When Looking for a New Car

If, after looking at all the used cars available in your area, you decide you want a new car after all and you plan to drive it forever—I've put more than 100,000 miles on my car in less than five years—you need to be aware of a few things.

Don't Splurge. Car dealers aren't in the business for their health, so they're going to try to tack everything on to that new car that they can—tilt steering wheel, cruise control, automatic windows and so on. These are all nice conveniences

◆◆◆

If you're trying to decide where to live, the most important things you can do are to trust only the Lord and to pray constantly. But even with prayer, you still have plenty of work to do.

◆◆◆

but certainly not worth the cost for someone who's having to watch dollars—pennies! So just stay with the essentials.

Do Negotiate. You aren't buying a loaf of bread with a fixed price. You're trying to get your best price on something that can be purchased for less than the sticker price. So go for it.

Ask Lots of Questions. And don't be timid about asking for sufficient information on those expensive "extras." When I bought my car in 1985, the young salesman tried to sell me a fabric protector package for $380.

I leaned forward and quietly asked, "What do they *actually* do?"

He gave me an elaborate song-and-dance about the importance of protecting the car's interior from spills.

I gave him the look I normally used on students who thought they were putting one over on "Ol' Lady Aldrich" and asked the question again. "But what do they actually do?"

He blushed, then stammered, "For four bucks, buy a can of Scotchgard™ and spray the seats."

I did exactly that.

Continue to Be Prepared *After* You Buy Your Car
How would you handle one of Colorado's sudden spring storms that can dump up to a foot of snow within a few hours? Even the threat of such an ordeal made me pack an emergency trunk kit.

In it I have a bag of cat litter in case I get stuck in an icy parking lot, a first aid kit, a flashlight and flashers, booster cables, road maps, simple tools, a can of instant flat-fixer, ice scrapers and ice grippers, a folding shovel and a pair of old boots.

The National Weather Service says I should also have a blanket or a sleeping bag, foil-wrapped matches, candles, paper towels, an extra coat, socks and gloves, nonperishable food such as peanut butter and Granola™, a compass and a pocket knife.

That's next week's car project.

Where to Live
If you think I've agonized over the purchase of a car, you should have seen me trying to decide where to live!

If you're in the same situation, the most important things you can do are to trust only the Lord and to pray—constantly. But even with prayer, you still have plenty of work to do.

When we were planning to move to Colorado Springs, I had only two afternoons to look for housing. But I'd been praying for a couple of weeks, so I knew the type of house we needed. I called Arlyene Ballard, the realtor who's since become my dear friend, and detailed both the house I wanted and the school district I wanted it in. She arranged for me to see 23 houses.

Our present home is the second place I looked at. As soon as I walked in, I *knew* it was my house. But I kept a straight face and let Arlyene show me all of the others. She teased me later about going through all that, but we both knew I had to see what was on the market.

When You're Looking to Buy
Since I've purchased two different homes in two different

places at two different times without even a good friend along, I want to pass along some of the things I've learned.

Do Your Homework First. Talk to school administrators, pastors and anyone else who will answer your questions. We were still living in New York when I started narrowing our choices for a school district, church and neighborhood in Colorado Springs.

The only people I knew in Colorado were Ron and Sharon Nothnagel, dear friends and former tennis partners. Even though they live in Boulder, about two and a half hours north of Colorado Springs, I wasn't bashful about calling them.

They knew one couple in Colorado Springs and suggested I talk to them. In turn, that couple suggested I talk to two teachers, who gave me the names of several others. By the time I finished the networking calls, I had a $302 phone bill, but I also had definite direction about which school I wanted Jay and Holly to attend, which church we'd join and which neighborhood we'd buy into.

Then Start Your Search. Work with a realtor from a reputable firm. Not only can she answer questions about the town, but she can also give you a list of mortgage companies and make arrangements for all inspections.

- **Insist on a structural inspection.** Face it, when we're under pressure, we have a tendency to make an emotional purchase, a kind of a I-could-just see-us-living-there reaction. That's valid certainly, but an inspection will eliminate doubts and problems that *will* crop up later when we're tired and wondering if we've made the right choice.

  The inspection will tell you the condition of the house and its foundation. Sure, it'll cost $100 to $200, but you'll know what you're buying and then you'll sleep better at night.

- **If you've run into a too-good-to-be-true deal, it probably is, so find out why.** Some homes, for instance, can't pass a radon inspection for natural radioactive gases, so the owners are willing to sell at a ridiculous price.

- **Check for cracks over the inside doors.** Such defects may mean the foundation has shifted.
- **Ask about the utility bills for the past year.** If they're higher than your new neighbors, you may have poor insulation.
- **Inquire about how the home is being heated.** And when was the furnace last cleaned and inspected?
- **Notice if the driveway is cracked.** Deep ones may signal that the ground is still settling.
- **Check to see if the roof is sagging.** If so, you may have a serious foundation problem.
- **Ensure that the water pressure is adequate.** To check the pressure, turn on the tap and then flush the toilet. The water flow in the tap should remain unchanged.
- **Don't assume anything!** Ask which appliances stay with the house. Include in your offer those appliances you want to buy with the house.

There! That's enough to get you started. Your library or local realty office will have more detailed information to help you feel more confident about your purchase. Remember, you *can* handle this, too!

When You're Looking to Rent

Okay, you've read this far and you're saying, "Sandra, come down to earth. Right now, on my income, buying our own home is out of the question. On my pay, I'm doing well just to meet current bills and to keep groceries on the table.

"But we do need a decent place to live. So tell me how to find a place to rent that I can afford."

Finding decent housing when you're a single mom with children and with limited means is not easy, particularly when many landlords insist, "No pets, no children." But, for what they're worth, here are some thoughts to get you started.

Find out What's Available. You need to know who does rent to families with children—with or without pets. Talk with others in your situation. Read the classifieds closely. Make inquiries.

And look into all types of housing: single-family homes, apartments, condos, whatever. I know you're already thinking *How Much?* but for the moment, don't worry if the rent for any of these places is out of your reach. Just find out if they'll accept kids.

Now, let's assume you found something suitable, and you can swing it on your income. Great, you're all set. But what if it's going to take two incomes to swing it? Then let's look at this next suggestion.

Team up with Another Single Mother. Have you found a nice place to live that's too expensive for one income? Or are you a divorced or widowed mother who's stuck with a house that you can't afford to keep by yourself? That latter circumstance is not all bad. Since you're already in the house, at least you don't have to come up with a security deposit plus first- and last-month's rent. You just need another single mom to share ongoing costs and responsibilities.

So, whether you've found something to rent that is beyond your means or are stuck with a place you can't afford to keep alone, have you advertised through your church, your place of work, the local supermarket bulletin board or the classifieds for another woman—ideally another single mom with kids—to share your home and expenses with you? Assuming you're compatible, you'll find that sharing a home with another mom and her kids has lots of benefits.

You'll have another adult companion in the home, so you won't be forced to live entirely in the world of children. You'll have someone to share chores, as well as expenses. And if you two can keep your social life and outside commitments flexible, each of you has a resident baby-sitter—without fees—for those times when you do have to be out of the home.

Consider Mobile Home Living. Check out mobile home parks in your area. Some are adult-only or seniors-only parks. But others are designed to be family parks. And, as a rule, whether to rent or buy, mobile homes—often called "coaches," but never "trailers"—cost much less than conventional housing of comparable size.

So even though you also have to pay a monthly lot rental to the park owners, the total monthly payment for coach and lot will frequently be well below the rental of even a tiny efficiency apartment. And, a single-wide coach can provide you with more bedroom space than many small apartments.

Generally, an attitude prevails in mobile home parks that benefits all who live there. Unlike residents in apartment complexes or in conventional neighborhoods, park residents tend to look upon one another as members of an extended family more than as neighbors. They look out for one another and help each other in times of need. Many life-long friendships develop in mobile home parks.

Also, many such parks offer activity programs that provide residents with a varied social life without leaving home, a real bonus in being able to get out from time to time without running up extra baby-sitting bills.

Check out Subsidized Housing. Federally subsidized housing is available in some areas for mothers and children with limited income. Such accommodation is a boon for the working mother who can, say, manage a month's rent, but cannot also come up with a security deposit and those formidable first- and last-month's rents at the same time. If you're in that situation, subsidized housing will provide you and the kids with suitable housing until they are older or until you can save enough for alternative accommodation.

Check with your nearest office of the Department of Housing and Urban Development to determine if you're eligible for their program. And even if you're eligible but have to go on a waiting list for a while because of lack of vacancies, it's still worth your while to get your name into consideration.

By now, you're probably coming up with ideas of your own. I wish you well in whatever option you chose for yourself and those kiddos of yours.

Once More with Feeling

- Always be prepared to avoid surprises and lemons.
- Regular maintenance will help you keep your cars for a long time. And you'll save money, if you learn to do the simple maintenance yourself.

- The more you understand about your car, the less frightened you'll be by it. Study your owner's manual and maybe take a course in basic maintenance.
- Know what to look for when you go to buy that used car. Then you will be less likely taken in by not-so-reputable salesmen and mechanics.
- Before you buy that used car, make sure the seller will agree to your having it checked out by your own mechanic.
- Call your insurance agent for his recommendation before buying any car, used or new. Your insurance can vary considerably depending upon year, make and model.
- Know how much you can afford. And once you've set that figure, don't let yourself be talked into spending "just a little bit more."
- If you're shopping for a house, be sure to do your homework first. Read everything you can and ask lots of questions.
- When you're buying a house, trust only the Lord. Work with a realtor from a reputable firm, insist on a structural inspection and don't assume anything!
- If renting a place to live is your option, find out first all that is available to families with children.
- If suitable housing is beyond your budget, team up with another single mom and rent a place together. If the two families are compatible, the arrangement offers many bonuses.
- Mobile home living and subsidized housing are other rental possibilities worth exploring.

EIGHT

AND WE'RE TO DO ALL THAT WITHOUT YELLING?

"No discipline seems pleasant at the time, but painful. Later on, however, it produces a harvest of righteousness and peace for those who have been trained by it."
HEBREWS 12:11

E arly in our adjustment as a family of three, eight-year-old Holly was mean to Jay, and she even refused rudely to complete a simple household task. Her obnoxious behavior continued through the morning until I finally gave her little bottom a couple of swats. She held back tears as she thrust out her lower lip, gave me one of her crushing looks and stomped upstairs.

I realize now that Holly was testing me, but at the time I felt defeated. After a few minutes, I quietly went upstairs to see about her. She was asleep on top of her bed, her arms wrapped around her dad's picture. Even though I had done the right thing, I felt terrible as I pulled a blanket around her tiny shoulders.

We've read enough from child experts to know that the purpose of discipline is to teach ultimate self-control as well as present acceptable behavior. We also know we're supposed to be consistent, issue reasonable punishment, make the rules clear and specific, criticize constructively and act promptly.

And we're to do all that without yelling?

Know Why You Discipline Your Children

So why do we moms struggle so? I'm convinced it's because we're often so busy with our own trauma that we merely *react* to our children, rather than thinking ahead and anticipating the problems that are likely to arise. Of course, helping our children develop self-discipline takes time and, since we never seem to have enough of that, all too many of us ignore the problems until they become crises.

But before we can expect our children to develop self-discipline we have to know *why* we desire it for them. One tired mother told me she'd always thought children were like little weeds—if you kept them fed, they'd just naturally grow. She's since discovered it takes much more than that.

So what do you want for your children? Remember Alice in *Alice in Wonderland* asking the Cheshire cat for directions? "Where do you want to go?" he asked her.

She answered, in bewilderment, "I don't know."

"Well, then," he said, "one way is just as good as another."

Have a Discipline Road Map

List Your Goals

To help me map out my discipline route, I've made an actual list of goals for my children. I want Jay and Holly to develop:

1. A close relationship with their heavenly Father.
2. Spiritual discernment.
3. A balanced view of money.
4. A servant's heart.
5. The ability to bounce back from a mistake—but to learn from the experience.

Define Your Values

Know your own values. If you aren't sure how to define those values, list all the things that are important and prioritize them. These head my list:

God,
Jay and Holly,
work,
extended family and friends.

To help me in that constant juggling between my family and God's work, I occasionally have to remind myself that if I'm sacrificing my children for the sake of "God's work," it's no longer God's work.

Establish Firm Limits

Set limits and stick by them. Teens are great howlers when it comes to rules, but they gain a sense of security if they know the limits.

But remember to communicate those expectations clearly. Teens don't like hearing "Well, you should have known that" any more than we do.

Build Self-esteem and Allow for Growth

Develop Their Self-esteem

Work on your children's self-esteem early. If a child feels good about himself, he will resist having to prove his worth through dangerous actions or inappropriate choices of friends.

Help your children find something at which they can excel. By developing positive skills, not only is self-esteem bolstered, but they aren't left with great blocks of unclaimed time. The adage "Idle hands are the devil's workshop" is true.

Let Them Grow

Let them grow. I have so many fears about the real world "out there," that I tend to want to keep my kids under my wing. But I've grown only when I was allowed to take responsibility, and I figure that's the only way my children are going to grow, too.

Reinforce Positive Social Development

Provide Group Experiences

Provide group experiences before the teen years. While you

still have the control, get your youngster involved in the church youth group or in a community organization. Of course, it takes time to chauffeur everyone here and there, but it can pay great dividends later.

Welcome Their Friends

Welcome your child's friends. You may feel as though you're fighting a never-ending battle against the power of the peer group. But it doesn't have to be that way.

Jay's and Holly's friends are welcome here, for then I'll know what they're doing. Admittedly, it takes time and

◆◆◆

Peer pressure can be almost overwhelming at times, and to resist such pressure may take more strength than some youngsters can muster....At such times, our kids need our support, not our rebuke.

◆◆◆

money to make our home available, but I'm convinced it's worth it.

Offer Your Kids Wide Shoulders to Lean On

Peer pressure can be almost overwhelming at times, and to resist such pressure may take more strength than some youngsters can muster. When that happens, your kids may break rules that you and they have already agreed upon. But these infractions are not so much acts of deliberate disobedience as they are manifestations of an inability to stand alone against one's peers and say no. At such times, our kids need our support, not our rebuke.

Be Supportive

I do remember how intense peer pressure can be, so while my own kids were in their early teens, I told them:

"When you're in a tough situation and you don't want the others to mock your decision, blame me.

Just say, 'I can't do that. My mom would kill me. And you've seen her; you know she's capable of doing exactly that.'

"My experiences through the years have given me broad shoulders; I'm happy to carry your challenges until you're strong enough to carry them yourselves."

In those early years, I was relieved to occasionally overhear one of them say into the phone, "Sorry, I can't. My mom won't let me" even though I hadn't been asked.

I'd always stroll past as though I was stone deaf. But inside I was rejoicing.

I taught high school for 15 years, so I enjoy being around teens. I love it when Jay and Holly invite their friends over to watch a video or play a board game. I supply the pizza, cheese and crackers, fruit and dip and brownies. Jay and Holly know the rules: they may invite whomever they want, but none of them may drink, smoke, swear or watch inappropriate movies in our home.

Admittedly, both my kids have some friends who make me a little nervous, but they are still welcome in our home. For many of them, this is a haven, and perhaps my rules give them an idea of what a structured family life—complete with regular dinner hours—is supposed to be.

Be Available

I don't hang around when the youngsters have their friends over, but I always "just happen" to be baking—the results of which are served fresh out of the oven—as Jay's friends stroll in. Of course, then I'm within earshot as I clean up the kitchen while the teens watch a video.

Only once have we had a problem. Holly had attended the school hockey game with a group of friends. I knew the driver of her car was responsible, so I allowed her to go, and then invited the whole gang back for pizza and a movie. I hadn't stressed they were going to watch a video I had chosen, so two of the guys brought back one they had rented.

I strolled through the family room on my way to the laundry (I always have towels that need folding). Immediately, I knew this was a movie I'd rather they not watch. Still, I hesitated to shut it off, not wanting to cause a scene.

Then in the midst of my wimpy decision-making process, *the* swear word came tearing out of the screen. Not only had I heard it, but the kids knew I'd heard it.

With the others looking out the corners of their eyes at me, I motioned for Holly to join me in the living room. Her "huh, oh" merely increased the tension.

But Be Firm

She followed me. "Well, Holly, you know the video is going to be turned off," I said. "Now would you like *me* to do that or would you rather take care of it yourself?"

Her eyes widened. Trying to save herself embarrassment, she muttered, "Mom! Like I don't hear that word—and worse—at school."

"Unfortunately you do," I answered. "But this is not school—this is our home. And you're not going to hear it within these walls. Now, again I ask: Do you want me to turn it off or are you going to take care of it?"

"You really are treating me like a baby."

And Be Diplomatic

She said it in such an uncharacteristically bratty way that I actually thought of slapping her. Instead, I had the good sense to wrap her in a bear hug.

"No, I'm treating you with the respect you deserve—exactly the way I expect your friends to treat you," I said. "If I thought you were a baby I would have thundered in there and turned it off myself. Out of respect for your maturity, I'm giving you the choice."

She went back into the family room and muttered, "Sorry, guys. My mom says we can't watch this."

I expected to hear groans from the group. Instead, one of the boys quickly apologized. "Oh, Holly, I'm sorry. We didn't mean to get you in trouble."

"I'm not in trouble. We just can't watch this."

Yes, my goal is to give my children a strong shoulder to lean against while they're learning their own balance.

Acquaint Your Kids with Your Work Environment

Including our children in our work and letting them see chunks of the adult world of work helps them to be less demanding.

Millie often takes her daughters to the office on Saturday while she runs off the financial forecasts for her company. As they help her put the reports into folders for a Monday morning meeting of the board, she tells them why the papers are so important. Not only do her girls see her work environment, but they are starting to understand how events elsewhere touch their own lives.

Whenever possible, I've included Jay and Holly in my article interviews, so they've learned early to fade into the background for those few minutes. Not only do they see how I pay the bills, but they've met some wonderful people.

One of their favorite adventures while "on assignment" with me occurred in Nashville, Tennessee in August 1988. I was tacking business onto our vacation and had arranged a magazine interview with someone I had long admired— Sarah Cannon, better known to Grand Ole Opry fans as Minnie Pearl.

On our way to meet Mrs. Cannon before her afternoon appearance on the Grand Ole Opry stage, I outlined her career to my teens, even retelling several of her down-home jokes in which she ridiculed her own looks. I explained the origin of those jokes, adding that she'd grown up being called "plain." Of course, to a child "plain" had translated as "ugly."

We waited only a few minutes in the reception area before Mrs. Cannon greeted us warmly. While she and I talked, Jay and Holly sat quietly, watching and listening.

Then, as we stood and thanked her, she took my hand and said in her quiet way, "Now, I want you and the children to sit out on the stage behind me."

Sit on the historic Grand Ole Opry stage? I nearly yelled aloud with glee, but managed to accept quietly. For the next two hours, the three of us sat behind many of the people who had been an important part of my growing up. Then, Mrs. Cannon, waiting behind the curtain for her cue, turned to smile at me as Roy Acuff announced, "Cousin Minnie Pearl!"

After the show, she graciously said good-bye to us and handed me her home phone number, so I could check details for the final draft of the article. Back at our car, Jay commented on the musicians, but Holly couldn't get over how attractive Mrs. Cannon is and wondered why she tells those awful jokes on herself.

Two weeks later, I made the prearranged call to Mrs. Cannon's home. I'd been professional all along, but as we said good-bye, she said in her gentle Southern voice, "Now do give my regards to your children. Jay and Holly, right?"

I was astonished that she had remembered them by name and said so. She commented, "My dear, they're remarkable children."

Right then I lost my professionalism and started to babble. "Mrs. Cannon, I have to tell you that after we left you at the Opry, Holly turned to me and said, 'Mom, she's so pretty!'"

Without missing a beat, Mrs. Cannon said, "Why, she's even more remarkable than I thought!"

Allow Consequences of Repeat Actions to Happen

Most of us have read the tough-love books telling us we must let our children experience the consequences of their actions, even if doing so means our discomfort in watching their discomfort. Learning by experience is the hard way to learn, but, for some youngsters, it is the only way.

Ginny had to bite her lip while letting her son spend his allowance unwisely and then—because she refused to bail him out—having to sit out several fun activities. She knew she was teaching him long-range lessons, but it was still tough to watch him miss out on important fun with his friends.

She could have rationalized giving him the extra spending money, especially since he had "already lost so much in life." But she wisely chose to have them both tough it out, so he would learn to budget his money better. It took a few rough weeks, but when he saw that his sorrowful eyes and pleas of "just this once" weren't working, he started watching his money more closely.

And I had to let Jay go to school without lunch several times as we were withdrawing from those good-ol'-Mom-will-come-through situations. When he'd been in elementary school, I'd often taken his lunch to him. But when we moved to New York at the beginning of his eighth grade, we agreed I wouldn't take his lunch to school anymore. Only occasionally did I find his lunch still in the refrigerator in the morning. Of course, he'd eat as soon as he got home at 3:00, so I knew his health wasn't in jeopardy.

Bend a Little on Minor First-time Offenses

Then the day came when I opened the refrigerator to get my lunch for work and discovered Holly had forgotten hers. Was it fair to treat her with tough love the first time she failed? But if I gave in, wouldn't I be teaching her that she didn't have to worry? That Good Ol' Mom would swoop in to rescue her?

I stood in front of the refrigerator for a long while, arguing with myself. Finally I decided that, if this became a habit, we'd deal with it then. I drove to her school, still mentally arguing with the tough-love experts, deciding Holly wasn't a candidate for their techniques just yet. Besides, I was going to suffer more than she would if I left her lunch in the refrigerator.

I arrived at school just a few minutes before her first class began. She and several of her friends were still by their lockers, combing their hair and chatting about the day's plans. Holly turned just as I approached. The look of surprise and pleasure on her face made the trip worth it. She thanked me profusely for bringing her lunch, reminding me she'd made egg salad and had been disappointed to discover she'd left it home.

Our long-standing custom has been to hug good-bye, but after I handed her the lunch and heard one more thank-you, I stood there awkwardly for a moment. I wanted that hug, but I didn't want to embarrass her in front of her friends.

Finally I said, "Well, I've got to head for work. Who wants a hug before I go?"

Kristi hopped up from the floor. "I do!"

I gave her a motherly bear hug, while Holly stood by, red-faced and saying, "Mom!"

Then Jessica said, "Me, too." One by one, I gave her five friends a squeeze to send them into the day. Finally only Holly was left. I hugged her and hurried out the door.

That night, as we cleared the table after dinner, she again thanked me for having taken her lunch to school. I said I hoped I hadn't embarrassed her with all of the hugs.

She shook her head. "You did at first because you're always doing weird things. But later, two of the girls said you're pretty neat. I just agreed with them."

I gave her another big hug right then.

When Push Comes to Shove, Hang Tough

While it's wonderful to be understanding, forgiving and open to discussing house rules, the time will come when you have to make a decision—and not let yourself be talked out of it. When those moments came for us, Jay and Holly used to argue.

But I'd say, "Just write this on your list of 'Rotten Things My Mom Used to Do' and show it to some future psychologist."

The argument always ended there.

Then came the year I decided we were going to attend an honest-to-goodness Fourth of July fireworks display. In the past, we'd always been at our lake place, and the kiddos had been content with sparklers. But this time I wanted to show them a sky filled with orange and green and red and blue. Okay, so *I* wanted to see a display again.

When I excitedly told them about my plans, they just glanced at each other with a here-we-go-again look. And that afternoon 10-year-old Jay ran into the house. "Mom! Timmy's got a bag of bottle rockets that we're gonna shoot off tonight. Isn't that great?!"

I looked up from my mending. "But we're going to the park to see the fireworks then. Remember?"

Jay frowned. "I don't wanna go. I wanna shoot bottle rockets."

For several moments I tried to reason with him. Finally I said, "That's enough. I'm pulling rank. You *are* going to the fireworks."

Jay glared at me and then went to his room.

All through dinner, he was sullen. At the park, he ignored my attempts to draw him into the conversation Holly and I were enjoying.

Then I opened the cooler. "What do you want? Cola or juice?" I asked, thinking he'd refuse rather than have to answer.

Instead he mumbled, "Cola."

I bit the inside of my lip to keep from commenting.

At last, the smoke rocket went up to test the degree of darkness. It was followed by an explosion that filled the sky with a brilliant orange umbrella.

As the crowd emitted a collective "ahhhh," Jay turned to me, his eyes sparkling. "Wow, Mom. This is great!"

My wink was the closest I got to saying, "I told you so."

Teach Your Children Responsibility

Counselors and child experts remind us that children who have time on their hands aren't happy. We know that those who have no chores and no responsibilities tend to quarrel much more than those who have to be busy around the home.

Also, single mothers easily get trapped into thinking they have to juggle *every* ball. But this one labeled "chores" can be easily passed along to the children. And we have the fewest discipline problems here when we make sure the kids understand exactly what we expect from them when we assign chores.

Usually we *can't* just say, "Clean your room."

We have to give specifics: "Make up your bed. Hang up your clothes. Put away the toys. Dust the dresser, chair and bed."

I've reminded myself of that fact many times when I've sent Jay back to his room with the thought that he is to look at the mess through *my* eyes. Let's face it, most teen boys just don't share their mother's obsession with a neat working area. I had to learn that Jay's room is Jay's room.

My kiddos liked having a list on the kitchen counter so they could cross off each item as they finished. I found that worked better than just giving them another chore after they'd finish the first one. If they kept getting a string of chores, they'd be defeated, thinking the work would never end. We all need to see that the goal is possible.

I also found they worked best if I worked with them. So

when they were first learning to work, I couldn't just say, "Put all your toys on the shelf." I needed to say, "*Let's* put your toys on the shelf."

Even young children can be in charge of an occasional meal that doesn't require cooking. And there's nothing wrong with chicken sandwiches for dinner.

The important thing is that you are spending time together and talking about your day. Meals together can often be the family's cement.

Naturally, I don't cook the way I used to—meat and potatoes on the table every night at 5:30—but I also refuse to give in to the fast-food syndrome. Our meals consist of a protein and a crunchy vegetable. And when I cook now, I make double portions so the leftovers—after getting zapped in the microwave—can provide another meal. I add a fresh salad, and we've got a feast.

One of our dinners each week is always baked chicken. Not only do we get a good meal, but the leftovers provide several lunches throughout the week. And that's a boon for me, as I refuse to buy regular lunch meat—it's too expensive and is filled with salt and nitrites.

Some good things have come out of my busy schedule— Jay and Holly have had to take more responsibility in the kitchen. The best system we've found is to alternate days of cooking and cleaning—Holly gets the even days and Jay gets the odd days.

Those first meals that the kids put together were rather interesting: Holly enjoyed trying cookbook recipes and trading ideas with her friends, while Jay served whatever was in the refrigerator. But he's progressed from warmed-over pizza to spicy potatoes and a marvelous cheese-broccoli soup. And we've all had a wonderful time.

Know When It's Time to Spank

Carl and Marilyn Amann, my Michigan friends with six children, were my parenting mentors long before my own Jay and Holly arrived. Carl said they punished biblically— warn, act, love.

Since we taught together for years, we often talked

about how difficult it was and is to raise little people. He insisted he couldn't use grounding as an effective tool with six, but said they knew that, after the paddling, he was going to wrap his arms around them until they both finished crying.

His wife, Marilyn, says, "It's neat to see our kids now making the same decisions we had to make"—such as no Saturday morning cartoons until each one's chores are done.

So hang in there and know that if we make the right decisions now we can relax—a bit—later.

Don't Let Discipline Become Abuse

Be Aware

Child abuse is a growing problem in our society. Whenever the growing statistics are cited, the same reasons are offered—stress, increased pressures, unrealistic expectations on the parent, frustration at the way life has turned out, alcohol and/or drug abuse, lack of an extended family support system or a continuing cycle of abuse from generation to generation. And the potential of abuse is often especially real for single mothers who are trying to juggle too many responsibilities.

I know how thin that line between discipline and abuse is. One day, early in my singlehood, we three were hurrying to get out the door to school and work. As they gulped their cereal, I hurriedly packed their lunch boxes since I'd been too tired the night before.

Then, just as we grabbed our jackets, 10-year-old Jay said, "Oh, I forgot. We're supposed to take our lunches in bags today since we're going to the museum."

I absolutely lost it. I slapped his arm in anger, then yelled about his thoughtlessness as I jerked the food items out of his lunch box and threw them into a bag.

They both watched—and listened—to me in stunned, frightened silence. Big tears welled up in Holly's eyes, and all Jay could say was, "I'm sorry, Mom."

I looked at those two frightened little kids who had no one to depend on except the crazy woman I had just become. I put my hands over my face and sobbed.

And that was exactly the right thing to do. Not only had I had the good sense to look at my children in that crazy scene and release my tension by crying, but that evening I also gave them the assignment of packing their own lunches.

Obviously, this was not an example of good discipline, but an example of a parent going over the edge.

Be Prepared

One of the joys of growing older is our ability to finally anticipate those situations that make us feel stressed out and hopeless.

If I'm overly tired or worried about bills or feeling pulled in too many directions, I'm impossible. But I've also learned to say, "I can't handle this well right now," and withdraw

◆◆◆

Children don't read minds any more than their parents do, so they aren't going to know they are loved unless they experience it through words and action.

◆◆◆

until I can cool down. And I know that, sooner or later, I'm going to have to talk to the Lord about it, so I try to talk to Him even while I'm still angry or disappointed.

Remember, when He said, "Come unto me," He *didn't* add, "But come with a smile on your face." It's as though He said, "Just haul it on in here. Let's talk."

Once I've had a time to cool off, I don't pretend nothing happened. I then have to face my kids, apologize and talk it through. But I don't wring my hands and lament that they have a rotten mother—because they don't!

Often I'll tell them what I need from them and what I'm willing to offer in return. Sometimes that translates into "When I get home from work, I need at least to get my coat hung up before you hit me with the latest crisis. Give me those few minutes, and I'll be ready to listen closely then."[1]

Serve Discipline with Love

I can't stress enough that discipline must be tempered with lots of love. Children don't read minds any more than their parents do, so they aren't going to know they are loved unless they experience it through words and action.

In the summer of 1987, I heard Dr. Gary Chapman, a pastor and counselor from Winston-Salem, North Carolina, speak on the five languages of love. Even though he was talking about husbands and wives seldom speaking the same language, his comments helped me understand Jay and Holly more.

Here are the five ways, he says, that folks hear they are loved:

Words. Hearing "I love you," "I appreciate your hard work" and "I'm glad you're part of this family" gives many of us the energy to tackle the next crisis.

Acts of service. The theme song for those with this language is "Don't Talk of Love—Show Me!"

Gifts. For many, Holly included, a gift often says, "I saw this and thought of you."

Physical Touch. Dr. Chapman says this is the language many husbands hear best. But translating that into a pat on your child's shoulder each time you pass or into a good-bye hug can convey your love, too.

Quality time. The amazing thing about this language is that this person, Jay included, wants to spend time with another but doesn't necessarily need to talk. Suddenly I understood those Southern husbands who wanted their wives to spend four hours fishing with them, but wouldn't utter nine words.

Of course, even though most of us speak one or two of these languages, a serving of a little bit of all of these will help us establish an atmosphere where the children know they are loved even as we keep working on the discipline.

Once More with Feeling

- Know why you discipline your children.
- Have a discipline road map in which you outline specific goals, define your values and establish the firm limits that give your youngsters a sense of security.

- Help build your children's self-esteem and aid their growth toward maturity.
- Reinforce their positive social development by providing suitable group experiences and making their friends welcome in your home.
- Discern whether your kids are being deliberately disobedient or simply caving in to peer pressure when they break agreed-upon rules.
- Acquaint your kids with your work environment to enhance their appreciation of your responsibilities and to broaden their horizons.
- Allow them to experience the natural consequences of repeated action.
- And be flexible where offenses are first-time and minor.
- But when push comes to shove, hang tough.
- Teach your children responsibility and keep them from idleness through assigned chores.
- Discipline biblically—warn, act, love. Don't allow discipline to become abuse.
- And always serve up discipline with generous amounts of love expressed in five different languages.

Note

1. By the way, for information and referrals of local protective agencies, you can write to: The National Committee for Prevention of Child Abuse, P.O. Box 2866, Chicago, IL 60690. Or call the National Child Abuse Hotline: 1-800-4-A-CHILD.

   To report child abuse locally, you can call the child protective agency in your county. Don't just close your eyes to what is happening to children. They need both the protection and discipline of loving adults.

We Love Our Kin, But We'll Raise Our Kids

"Do not forsake your friend and the friend of your father, and do not go to your brother's house when disaster strikes you—better a neighbor nearby than a brother far away."

PROVERBS 27:10

Remember Aesop's fable about the man who tried to please everyone? He and his son were on their way to market, leading their donkey and enjoying the beautiful morning together.

One of their neighbors saw them and said, "Now isn't that silly? You have a fine donkey with you, but both of you are walking."

So the father set his son on the donkey, and they continued toward the market.

But after a few minutes, another friend saw them and said to the son, "How rude you are to ride while your old father must walk."

So the father joined the child on the donkey's back. It wasn't long, though, until they passed a third friend.

"How thoughtless you are," he said, "to make this poor donkey carry both of you to town."

So they both slid off the donkey, and the father promptly picked up the animal and put it across his shoulders.

As they slowly walked along, a fourth neighbor saw them. "Well, that's the most stupid thing I've ever seen—a donkey being carried."

The obvious moral is that we can't please everyone. May we apply that same philosophy to our single parenting.

We Will Care for the Children

When I made that conscious decision not to marry again— contrary to the comments and advice of my relatives—I also made the decision that I would raise Jay and Holly to the best of my ability—alone. Again, my decision ran contrary to the expectations of my relatives.

A typical Kentuckian, my dad is a teller of tales, and most of his accounts of life in the hills are filled with high drama. I grew up listening, horrified and in tears, to epics of a neighbor murdering his wife, of children being given away or of a fire consuming wooden houses within minutes.

But the story he told of his grandfather John T. Dunn's refusal to accept his second wife's children always stirred my temper rather than my tears.

John T's first wife had died, leaving him with three youngsters. Grief and reality often walked together in the hills at the turn of the century, so within a matter of weeks, he was looking for another wife to take care of his children. The prime candidate was his first cousin Sis—a widow with three young boys. They married quickly, and the boys were sent to live with Sis's brother in a neighboring town.

When the mule-drawn wagon with the three boys in it started down the lane away from the only house they knew as home, the youngest began to scream out, "Mama! Mama!"

When Dad mentioned the little boy's grief at being separated from his mother, I went berserk.

"How could she give up her children like that?"

"What do you mean?" Dad asked. "John T's house was too small for three more boys."

"But not too small for the ones he and Sis had together

afterwards! I'd be cussed before I'd give up my children like that!"

"What would you do?" he'd ask. "There you are stuck in the hills with three young'ns, living off other people's charity."

At 17, I had more fight than sense. But I also had mother bear instincts, and I knew even then I'd fight for my cubs.

"We'd walk to the nearest town even if it took days," I said. "I'd find work or I'd walk the streets, but I'd feed my children. And no man on this earth would take 'em from me!

"Sis was spineless for giving hers up, and John T was scum for making her do so!"

Neither of us ever won over the other when it came to airing our views on his grandparents and their kids. But I did learn one rule when arguing with Dad—never to call his favorite relatives names.

That argument between Dad and me over John T and Sis was 20 years old when my husband died. And suddenly then, my dad took comfort from our long-standing battle. He knew Jay and Holly—his grandchildren—would be well taken care of.

We Will Decide What's Best for Them

After Karen became a widow, her father-in-law started complaining about her keeping the two children in a Christian school and, as he said, "shielding them from the real world."

She was convinced that was best for the children for a while. So like Hannah in 1 Samuel 1:15—when the priest Eli accused her of being drunk—she quietly answered the charges.

"I know you're concerned as a loving grandfather," she said. "But I'm the one who's responsible for them. I'm the one who must stand before God and give an account."

Later, she talked with a trusted friend about her frustrations, saying through her tears, "It's a bigger issue than just the public or private school matter. It's the whole thing of whether I know what's best for *my* two children."

I can identify with that feeling, because some of my relatives had quiet fits when I moved to New York. They'd never been there themselves; they had only seen movies of

New York City. But they told me I was taking my children into one of the world's roughest spots.

As it turned out, only the financial part was rough. I loved the cloistering tree branches that hung over the road there and the gentle rolling hills that reminded me so much of my own beloved Kentucky. And I was especially pleased with the schools.

So I shrugged off the relatives' comments. By the time I'd decided to move away from their cocoon, I'd stopped trying to please them.

We Are Still in Charge

Not only do relatives expect us to act a certain way, but those expectations easily fall onto our children. Two days after my husband's funeral, his dad said good-bye to us in our kitchen.

As he hugged 10-year-old Jay, he said, "Take care of your mother. You're the man of the house now."

I was standing where I could see Jay's face, and I was struck by the panic that flashed across his eyes.

I looked at his grandfather. "No, Dad. He's still the 10-year-old son in this house."

Jay has since commented at how much it meant to him that I'd say that. He'd just lost one parent; he needed the security of knowing that his mom was in charge.

We Won't Worry Anymore About Fitting an Image

I guess I knew I shouldn't have cared quite so much about what all the relatives think. But for a long while I did.

It's been difficult to swim against the emotional tide—and standards—they set for me during those early years when I was growing up. Besides, adults are just tall children, and there's enough little kid in me that I've always wanted my extended family to be proud of me.

In the 1950s, when I was growing up within my Southern subculture, I was supposed to learn to care for a future family. That translated into planting enormous vegetable gardens, canning and freezing the produce, sewing my own clothing and making quilts from the leftover fabric. Those are certainly admirable skills, but they didn't mesh with my determination to go to college and become a teacher.

Naturally, at the obligatory clan gatherings, I felt like a misfit as an occasional uncle commented on my getting "too proper" or one of many aunts pointedly praised her daughter's latest sewing project before asking what I was working on. Gradually, I got it into my head that I wouldn't be a "real woman" until I made my own quilt.

Trying to Fit My Relatives' Image

So, within a week of graduation from college, I purchased a kit for a white quilt top that I was to embroider with shades of blue before quilting it with several thousand tiny stitches

◆◆◆

**I've learned along the way what is really important:
to keep my eyes on Him and off the impossibility
of fitting into the images and expectations of others.**

◆◆◆

into a scroll pattern. I worked on it, off and on, while I completed my master's degree and produced two babies. Finally, six years later, the day came when my quilt was finished.

I invited my Kentucky grandmother, Mama Farley, my mother and two of my aunts for an official showing that would declare my womanly status at last. I spread the quilt across a double bed and stood back, awaiting their verdict.

Mama Farley smiled. "Oh honey, that's pretty. That's just about the prettiest I've ever—"

She stopped in midsentence as she turned back the corner of the quilt to examine its underside. Then suddenly, she let it fall back onto the bed.

"Oh! Knots!" was all she would say.

Why hadn't I remembered that the knotted thread must always be pulled into the inside of the quilt? I hadn't, so I still wasn't a "real" woman.

I had no choice but to try again. For my next quilt, I chose a pink dogwood pattern to be appliqued onto a white background. That one took me nine years of sewing tiny stitches as I taught, raised children, wrote books, nursed my husband through numerous cancer battles, grieved his death and, later, moved my children to New York for my career change.

One Saturday morning, I finished the pink binding and knotted the last of the pink thread—remembering to tuck it inside. Jay and Holly were at an overnight youth activity, so, alone in our small condo and 800 miles from any relatives, I spread the quilt onto my bed, turned back the corner to check for knots and pronounced myself a real woman—at long last!

Learning to Keep My Eyes on the Lord
Actually, by then, the ceremony had lost its earlier meaning because my having survived the traumas of grief and a career change had already convinced me I wasn't quite as worthless as I had once thought. I was learning to release my low self-esteem to the Lord and to latch onto Philippians 3:13,14: "But one thing I do: Forgetting what is behind and straining toward what is ahead, I press on toward the goal to win the prize for which God has called me heavenward in Christ Jesus."

Oh, I've hit a few bumpy spots in the process, but I've learned along the way what is really important: to keep my eyes on Him and off the impossibility of fitting into the images and expectations of others.

We'll Just Ignore the Demands of Others
In that first year of trying to juggle emotions and adjustments along with the relatives' demands, I poured out my frustration to long-time friends, Dan and Janet Pope.

Dan listened in his quiet way, and then gave me the best advice any single parent could have: "Walk in God's light and pay no attention to what the rest of us say."

Once More with Feeling
- As a single mom raising kids alone, you can't hope to satisfy the expectations of all your relatives, so don't even try to.
- You, not they, someday will stand before God to give an account for your parenting, so resist their attempts to

pressure you in directions that are not best for you and the children.

- So stand firm in your decision to care for them and to decide what is best for them.
- But don't make things worse with an offending relative by arguing. Remember the truth of Proverbs 15:1: "A gentle answer turns away wrath, but a harsh word stirs up anger."
- In the absence of a father, protect your small children from feeling unduly burdened. They need the security of knowing that mom is still in charge.
- Remember to keep your eyes on Him and off the impossibility of fitting into the images and expectations of others.
- Walk in God's light and pay no attention to what all the rest are saying.
- Listen to the Lord and you'll find the voices of relatives growing softer.

WHEN THE KIDS FIGHT

"How good and pleasant it is when brothers live together in unity!"
PSALM 133:1

Jay and Holly used to have the most ridiculous arguments. One day, I'd just gotten home from work when they stormed into my bedroom.

"Mom, ground Holly," Jay demanded. "She threw stuff at me!"

"Holly," I asked, "what did you throw at him?"

"String," she conceded.

I sighed and looked at Jay. "What's the big deal? So she threw string at you."

He never batted an eye. "Mom, it was on a *spool*."

Kids Will Fight, but Hang in There

We single mothers have enough crises to juggle without having to referee within our own homes. But having our children at odds often happens.

I remember all too well the tension that Jay and Holly—"the greatest kids in the world"—went through as both often wished each were an only child. And there were moments when, if they'd kept it up, I could have accommodated either wish very easily!

At times, I was convinced they stayed awake nights, thinking up ways to aggravate each other. That started just about puberty—and it was an exhausting time.

For a while, they were so rude to each other that I was tempted not to write this book. One exhausting afternoon I listened to another round of "Did not. Did, too," until I said, "Boy, my editor ought to hear this. How can I write about single parenting when you guys don't get along?"

Jay barely glanced my way. "Just have a chapter called 'When the Kids Fight.'"

I shook my head. "But we've been through so much together! And we've got enough battles outside; we don't need to face more *inside* these walls! We've got to get through this as friends!"

Simultaneously, they looked at each other and laughed. So much for manipulation by guilt.

For It Will Get Better

Having Rules Helps Some

When their quarreling first appeared, I had two rules:

Rule One: No battles—either physically or verbally.
Rule Two: You don't have to like one another, but you do have to respect each other.

They didn't always stick to those rules, but just knowing I expected that behavior helped keep them on track. I'm convinced youngsters will eventually meet our expectations, so I tried to say encouraging things such as "You're a neat kid. I'm surprised you said anything that mean."

But Their Maturity Helps Most

They're in their late teens now and friends again. In fact, when we were out in the car recently, Holly said, "You know, Mom, Jay's really neat. I like talking to him."

I almost wrecked the car as I whipped around to see who'd said that.

Now that Jay and Holly are older, we're wonderfully on the other side of the problem. They talk, occasionally double-date and even run errands together. I stand by the front window, waving good-bye and marveling that they're friends again.

How did it happen?

If I knew *exactly*, I'd go on a packed-house lecture tour.

Oh, I want to take credit and say that my involvement with my teens, my demand for mutual respect and our constant communication brought us to this refreshing understanding. But, in reality, their maturity had more to do with it than anything else.

When Do Kids Fight?

If your children are still little, when do they argue? Always, of course, when it's the most inconvenient or awkward for you. Kids can square off anytime at the drop of a hat, but these times seem to rank among their favorites for sparring with one another:

Whenever the Phone Rings

Every mother knows that as soon as the phone rings and she goes to answer it, kids look at each other and say, "What can we get into? I know; let's fight."

One young mother keeps special games by the phone that the children can play with only when the phone rings. That's solved a big problem.

Just Before the Evening Meal

Others discovered their kids fight in that hour before dinner. Sheila has a system now that as soon as she gets home from work, her youngsters can make the dinner salads and have those to eat right away. Some moms keep sliced carrots and quartered apples handy.

Yes, it takes time to make sure those items are available but—since most kids prefer eating to arguing—it keeps the children from feuding and lets the moms change out of their work clothes without first having to referee another unscheduled bout.

When You're the Most Tired

With my kids, it seemed that the biggest arguments started when I was the most tired. So I would ask them to suggest their own solutions for solving the current difficulty.

Holly's suggestions were invariably the most reasonable, and Jay's were always the most dramatic. But, between them, they usually managed to get us through the crisis of the moment.

More on this point later.

And Always in the Car

My two youngsters have vastly differing tastes in music, so, in the car, it seemed as soon as we had finished praying for journeying mercies, but were still in the driveway, they were already arguing over the radio stations.

My standard solution was uncreative, but it worked. "If you two can't agree on what station to listen to, you'll just have to listen to the one I want."

They quickly learned that listening to my music was worse than listening to each other's, so they compromised.

Why Kids Fight

They're Trying to Establish Their Own Identity

I've found that teens are often at odds because they're trying to pull away from the family unit to establish their own identity. That's tension enough, but add a sibling or two going through their own crises and you've got the potential for a battle.

They're Feeling They Don't Have a Voice in Anything That Happens

Part of the frustration of being a child is not having a voice in anything that happens. This feeling is particularly strong in a child who is being expected to take care of all the others.

Patty remembers always having to take care of three

younger brothers and never feeling as though she had a voice in anything that was happening in her life. No wonder she couldn't wait to get out of that house. And sadly, she isn't close to any of her family now.

When her mother wants to have the whole family together at holidays, Patty tries to avoid it, thinking *I had enough of that when I lived with them.*

How to Keep the War Going

Yell a Lot

When they're arguing again, the easy thing to do is yell, "Shut up!" but that merely increases the tension—and the volume.

◆◆◆

Even saying something to toddlers as seemingly innocent as, "Let's see who is Mommy's best helper," while you and the children pick up their toys creates competition. Unintentionally, you make them rivals, not for a prize, but for Mommy's favor and approval.

◆◆◆

Go for Guilt

One thing that doesn't work with kids is trying to make them feel guilty for not liking each another. Sue remembers her mother saying, "Just think if something happened to your brother and sister." She says she thought about that a lot.

When Jay and Holly used to argue, I'd remind them that no one else on this earth shares the same memories as the two of them.

"Years from now," I'd say, "no one else will know how you got Petey Cat; no one else will remember the guy Jay nicknamed "Fredetals"; no one else will have shared the same experiences with our zany relatives."

Set Up Competition

A principle every parent in the world knows but doesn't always follow is *don't set up competition,* especially the kind that generates antagonisms and turns your kids into adversaries. We know we have enough problems without pitting our children against each other, so we think, *I'd never do that.*

But even saying something to toddlers as seemingly innocent as, "Let's see who is Mommy's best helper," while you and the children pick up their toys creates competition. Unintentionally, you make the children rivals, not for a prize, but for Mommy's favor and approval.

Make Comparisons

Grades are a common problem area, and more than one adult still remembers hearing, "Why can't you get good grades like your sister?"

I confess here that I wish Jay had more of Holly's neatness. But I try to stay out of comparisons. Once a much-younger Holly said, "I bet you wish Jay was neat like me, huh, Mom?"

I fought the impulse to say "Yes!" Instead I praised her and then pointed out some of Jay's good qualities: "Holly, I'm so glad you keep your room neat. That really helps give me a sense of peace and harmony. Jay doesn't keep his room neat, but I do appreciate his helping me paint the kitchen without my having to bug him."

How to Win a Cease-fire

Involve Them in the Solutions

At home, since the biggest arguments seemed to start when I was the most tired, I usually asked the kiddos for their own suggestions: "How would you solve this one if you were the mom and I was the child?"

Holly always suggested reasonable solutions. "I guess I'd send us to separate rooms until we can decide to get along."

Jay would be dramatic. "No, remind us how difficult it is to raise kids alone. Remind us that you didn't run away to Tahiti or to Kentucky when Dad died and tell us how Grandmaw Sis gave her children up when she married John T. And we'll remind you that their youngest boy wouldn't even go to his mother's funeral years later."

By the time he'd finished, I was usually laughing so hard that the tension was gone from the situation.

Keri asked her 10-year-old son how he'd solve their argument and was surprised to hear him say, "I'd ask the kid what had happened at school that day that made him so grouchy."

Give Each Separate Time

With two totally different children, I've found that spending separate evenings together works for us. So, while Holly's baby-sitting, Jay and I often go out for hamburgers and talk. Then when Jay's working, Holly and I shop or chat over quiche at our favorite tea shop.

I shared my idea with a young friend who promptly told me that families are stronger as they do things together—always. I also noticed her children weren't even five years old yet!

But the separate times work for us. Just as children need personal space—whether it's a room or just a brightly-colored "secrets" box—they need to have their parent for a few minutes that belong just to them alone. In fact, if children know they'll have uninterrupted time later, they're less apt to be so demanding beforehand.

Treat Them as Individuals

As their mother, I try to treat Jay and Holly fairly and equally. But I can't and don't treat them the same, because they aren't the same. When Jay has a problem, he wants to be left alone until he's worked it out mentally. Then he'll run his decision by me.

Holly, on the other hand, involves me in every detail of her working-through process. By the time she's made her decision, we're both tired.

Sure, it's exhausting trying to treat them as individuals, but so's trying to undo the damage from trying to raise cookie-cutter kids.

And speaking of equality: Do your children ever argue about which one should get the larger half of the last piece of cake? Mine used to—until I heard a veteran mother say that she solved the problem by having one child cut the coveted item and by giving the other child first choice.

Get It in Writing

Just as the contract Holly had written about dating got me

out of many rough spots, so have the other contracts that the kids and I have drawn up concerning curfew, grades and social life. Not only do they clarify any misunderstandings, but they help me remember what I've said.

Achieve an Armistice with Prayer

Several years ago, it'd been another one of those frustrating days when I didn't need to face two warring teens. As soon as I hit the door, though, they both wanted to tell their side of the story—namely whose turn it was to get the TV.

Understanding mother that I am, I spouted something close to, "You guys must hold secret meetings at night to see how you can drive me nuts!"

I didn't even have my coat off yet, but we sat on the carpeted stairs as I listened to one side and then to the other. Then I mumbled, "I gotta pray about this."

Still on the stairs, I started with a simple, "Father, I hate days like this. I identify more with Saul's craziness than Solomon's wisdom, so please show me how to solve this."

Jay and Holly didn't offer to pray then, and I didn't make them. They needed space and time to think. I sent them to their rooms, said they couldn't watch TV for the rest of the evening and added that I didn't want to see them until dinner, 30 minutes later. We'd work out a schedule then.

At a mothers' luncheon some time later, I shared my honest prayer. Later another mother scolded me for *not* making my children pray aloud right then. She declared that she does that all the time and her children never even raise their voices in the house.

She also let me know that, if I were a truly spiritual mother, my children would have done the right thing immediately.

I asked her how old her children are.

"Six and nine," she answered.

I patted her arm. "That's wonderful," I said.

But what I meant was "Let's talk again in about seven years."

Keep Working for Peace

Truthfully, I don't want my children to be mechanically obedient little robots. I want children who are learning how to work through problems and who see God as their heavenly Father to whom they can go, whether they're hurting or happy.

Maybe, just maybe, by seeing me turn to the Lord for solutions, my kiddos will learn that He's ready to listen to anything.

Once More with Feeling

- Hang in there; it will get better. Having rules helps some; but the children's own maturity—which takes time to achieve—helps most.
- Don't be surprised that your kids seem to pick the most awkward times possible to argue. In fact, you can count on it.
- Watch to see when your children argue most. Once you've identified those times, find creative ways to head them off.
- Driving you crazy is seldom your kids' intent when they fight. More often, they're only trying to establish their own identities or they may be feeling they don't have anything to say in what is going on around them.
- You can keep your youngsters fighting by such counterproductive steps as yelling a lot, going for guilt, creating competition of the wrong kind and constantly making unfortunate comparisons between the kids.
- Listen to your children's complaints. You may see another facet of the problem.
- Involve them in the solutions to their problems. Even an off-the-wall suggestion may provide the right result.
- Give each child time alone with you. Knowing they can count on those uninterrupted minutes when you are entirely theirs adds peace to the household.
- Do treat your children as individuals with separate interests and different needs. They are not the same, so you can't treat them the same, even though you are being fair and giving each one equal consideration.
- Pray honestly for them and with them. "More things are wrought by prayer than this world dreams of." (Tennyson)
- As your children see you turn to the Lord for solutions, they will learn to see God as their heavenly Father to whom they can also go, whether they're hurting or happy.

ELEVEN

HELP, WHEN I TIED MY SON'S TIE HE TURNED BLUE!

"I thank my God
every time I remember you."
PHILIPPIANS 1:3

everal years ago, Jay, Holly and I shared a tour bus with a group from Mexico City. We couldn't communicate with them, but we smiled and nodded at each other, as our guides explained the various historical sights.

It was a long day, and by the time our bus stopped for dinner, I was exhausted. As we lined up for the washroom, I rested my arms on top of Holly's head, thinking of the day's endless activities.

I had been cheated in the purchase of a cameo. I had momentarily lost Jay twice. I had tripped over Holly all day—she insisted on being as close as possible to avoid the men who insisted on pinching her rosy cheeks. Basically, I thought I'd made a mistake in taking the trip.

Then one of the Mexican grandmothers stopped in front of me, patted my arm and said, "You good mama."

Suddenly, I wasn't quite so tired.

We All Need Each Other

Yes, we all need encouragement, and sometimes we find it in unusual places. But even with all my needs, it's been difficult for me to accept help graciously. Then on a trip to the Middle East, I learned we all need each other.

In Old Jerusalem, the cavelike shops with their piles of spices and fruits, camel rugs and rows of carved manger scenes delighted me. But it was the people who interested me most. We bumped against one another in the narrow passageways, my murmured "Sorry" falling meaningless on ears that comprehended no English.

Just in front of the slabs of beef and lamb in the open-air meat market, I saw a young Palestinian mother. Cradled in her left arm was a baby, just a few months old. With her right hand, she was steering a little boy about three years old. Even though her long gray-green dress and white head scarf bespoke her different culture, I thought of my own days of juggling two babies and several purchases.

Just then a collective groan went up as the people began moving to the sides of the street. That's when I saw the garbage tractor inching toward us. The streets were already crowded—how could the driver get that tractor through here?

But still I moved aside with the crowd, muttering my usual "Sorry." The unrelenting tractor advanced upon us, forcing us to flatten ourselves—four deep on each side—against the storefronts and each other. Slowly, it began to crawl past us, its oversized tires only millimeters from my back.

Suddenly someone was pummeling my legs. The little son of the Palestinian mother was trying to fight his way past me—and into the path of that awful tractor with its load of garbage.

I grabbed his shoulder and looked beyond the tractor to where I had last seen the young mother, knowing the panic she must feel. She also was trapped against the wall, clutching the baby close to her face to keep the child from being crushed. But while she was protecting the one, her eyes were darting over the crowd for the other who had been separated from her in the pushing.

Still gripping her little son's shoulder with one hand, I

waved to her with the other while her little boy clung to my tired knees for all he was worth.

"He's here. I have him here with me!" I shouted.

Her bewildered stare let me know she didn't understand me, and all of us were pressed too tightly together for me to pick the child up for her to see. All I could do was point dramatically toward my feet and give an okay sign, hoping she understood that her son was safe.

At last, with the garbage tractor safely behind us, I could steer the child to his anxious mother. As he recognized her skirt, he clutched it, sobbing with relief. I touched his dark hair and looked into the brown, misty eyes of his mother as she nodded her thanks to me.

I wanted to tell her about my two children. But we couldn't talk; we merely looked at one another through our tear-filled eyes. I touched her little boy's head just once more and then slipped back into the throng of shoppers.

I had been there for that mother's child during a time of crisis. And we, as single parents, quickly learn that we need others to be there for our children, too.

And We All Need Help

Help Can Come from the Lord

I've noticed that when I ask the Lord for a pat on the back, He's quick to give it. But not always in the way I expect.

I remember one Michigan Saturday that wasn't going well at all. I was having trouble balancing the checkbook and my mechanic said the rocker arm—whatever that is—on the car had to be replaced.

I wanted to run away but settled for taking the three of us out for hamburgers. As we walked into the restaurant, I saw that one of my former students—I'll call her Donna—was a waitress there.

Oh, good, I thought sarcastically, *I'm tired and discouraged and I run into one of the most obnoxious students I've had in 15 years of teaching.* I could still see her in the front row of fifth-hour mythology, arms folded and eyes daring me to make the lesson interesting.

But I wasn't going to disappoint Jay and Holly by going to another restaurant. I decided I'd just pretend I hadn't seen her. *Well, Lord, just keep us from being seated in her section, please,* I prayed inwardly.

And where did the hostess led us? Right to Donna's section, of course. *Any place but here,* I told myself. But just as I opened my mouth to ask for a booth near the window, Donna spotted us and came rushing over.

"Mrs. Aldrich! This is so neat!"

Sure, it'll be easier to poison me this way, I thought. But outwardly, I managed a feeble smile.

◆◆

A good church is the only thing that's going to see our kids through the rough times. Oh, we have no guarantee that church involvement will keep them out of trouble, but our chances for survival are much better.

◆◆

"Guess what!" she said. "I'm a Christian now!"

I stood there dumbstruck as my mouth dropped open.

Donna just kept bubbling on. "My sister got saved at college," she said. "And it bugged me that she was always witnessing to me. Then I'd go to your class, and you'd compare the Bible to what the Greeks believed, and I'd get angry all over again.

"But I couldn't get what you said out of my mind. And last year, I got saved! Isn't that neat?"

I was too choked up to talk, so I could only give her a hug.

Help Can Come from the Church

That's the first step. We can't always depend on our families to provide the encouragement we need, especially if we're clear across country. And, by this time, many of our friends are hurting from the same circumstances.

A good church is the only thing that's going to see our kids through the rough times. Oh, we have no guarantee that church involvement will keep them out of trouble, but our chances for survival are much better.

When we moved to Colorado Springs, our furniture wasn't due to arrive until Monday. But that Sunday before—and only two days after we arrived in town—we were in church.

I'd already talked to several people about the local churches. We'd been in a small fellowship in New York that had provided exactly the sense of family we needed. But with our new move we wanted a bigger church that could offer a wider range of activities.

I quietly checked on the youth leaders, but one of my California friends, Patricia, was more direct after her divorce. She went to the youth minister at their church and told him he had a marvelous opportunity to make a difference in her then nine-year-old son's life. She asked if he was willing to accept the challenge.

He was, and for the next several years he and her son, Kelly, met often for Saturday breakfast. Patricia credits him for helping steer a lonesome boy through the difficult teen years. But none of that would have happened if she hadn't gathered the courage to tell someone what she needed.

Help Can Come from the Kids

Youngsters also can lighten their mom's load—in their own way. A few months after Jay turned 13, he heard me tell one of my friends that I'd appreciate her prayers as the date of what would have been my twentieth wedding anniversary loomed.

The kiddos' dad had promised me that, for the Big Two-O, he would ask me to marry him, so I dreaded facing that lonely time.

You see, Don had never asked me to marry him. Years ago, when we were still students, he had simply *told* me we were getting married at semester break. And we did.

But that night, after Jay and Holly went to bed, I worked at my desk. Soon Jay meandered into my office, stammered another "Good night, Mom" and wandered out. Within five minutes, he had done that twice more.

Finally, I said, "Jay, what *is* it?"

He shuffled from one foot to the other in that embarrassed way common to young teens.

At last he blurted, "Mom, will you marry my dad?"

Softly, I answered, "You bet I will, Jay."

Help Can Come from Neighbors and Friends

When we still lived in Michigan, Jay had to wear a tie for his spring concert. Neither one of us had the foggiest notion how to tie a four-in-hand, so I asked a neighbor to teach him. The neighbor did, bless him, and Jay was set for his concert.

During the Vietnam War, I heard of a young mother who was having trouble potty training her two-year-old son. Her husband was in the army, and none of her male relatives were close by to give the little guy an example of how to tackle this latest milestone. So she confided to her neighbor and, with some embarrassment, stammered her request for help.

As a result, each evening for the next couple of weeks, she took her son to the neighbor's house, so the husband could give the little fellow a lesson. It worked!

Dr. James Dobson, the renowned Christian psychologist, has another idea: drop colored ice cubes in the toilet bowl and encourage the little guy to fire away. That works, too!

Help Can Come from the Experts

In 1986, when Jay was 13, I was struggling with finding the balance between letting him have fun and forcing him to be, as he put it, "a wimp."

The scene was one of those this-business-of-raising-kids-alone-is-tough episodes. We were still in Michigan then, and Jay had come in from the lake all excited about this wonderful new game he, Erik and Andy had of jumping out of a moving boat.

Horrified, I gave the typical, teary-mother arguments about the danger of what he was doing. But he said he could "handle it."

At that point, I launched into an account of Steve, a brilliant former student, who had been killed in a freak accident at his college. I even told about one of our distant relatives who had been killed by his own boat motor when he fell into the lake.

Still, Jay remained insistent that he and his friends

would be fine. I was just worrying too much, he told me.

Then in a sudden burst of inspiration, I called the Coast Guard, explained the situation and asked if I was overreacting. The officer assured me I wasn't and said that not only were the boys' activities stupid, but they were a good way to get killed.

I asked if he'd tell Jay what he had just told me. They talked for quite a while. As far as I know, the boys didn't play the game again.

That call may very well have saved young teens' lives. Sometimes we have to do the hard thing for the future good

◆◆

It's ironic—and maddening at times—but kids often will receive counsel from others that they will not accept from their parents.

◆◆

of a youngster—whether it's calling a counselor or the police.

It's ironic—and maddening at times—but kids often will receive counsel from others that they will not accept from their parents. You know how that goes: Good ol' Mom's nice to have around sometimes, but really, what does she know?

So whatever the need is and whenever it's necessary, don't be afraid to bring in the heavy artillery.

But Help Comes Only When We Ask

Whatever our need, we must stop waiting for others to anticipate and fill it. They don't read minds any more easily than we do. So, instead of whining, "Nobody understands how rough I have it," we must ask for specific help from our church, from a friend, from whomever when we need it.

Remember, if you don't ask, the answer is *always* no.

In the early days of our singlehood, it's often difficult to find the balance between letting friends help and leaning on them. I was fortunate to have emotional support in those early days, so gradually I got my footing and moved on.

Often, though, when well-meaning friends said, "Call me if you need anything," I failed to do so.

Why?

I had so many needs I didn't know where to begin. I wish I'd been able to verbalize my needs *then*.

Here's how I, and other single moms like me, can be helped:

Pray for Me

I may appear strong, but the load of single parenting and career juggling is heavy. If I'm new to this role, I'm struggling with unfamiliar territory and need all the help I can get.

If the Lord gives you specific direction, please listen. He knows my needs—whether it's for help with grocery money or for someone to take my son to the Father/Son Banquet at church.

Talk to Me

When you see me in church, please offer a sincere greeting. If my children are small, I'm especially hungry for adult conversation. I often feel awkward in church, and your smile and greeting on Sunday morning will make a big difference.

When you ask how I am, please hang around for the answer. If you'll take an interest for even a few minutes in what I'm doing, I won't feel so alone—and I won't be so demanding of your time.

And please remember that accepting a divorced person isn't the same as condoning divorce.

Extend Common Courtesy to Me

Every single woman can tell about being asked at a banquet to move to another seat because a couple wanted to sit at a particular table. Not only is the request rude, but it tells the single woman that in the eyes of others, she's second-rate.

And please don't talk about your couples' gatherings in front of me. I may be reading the bulletin board in the cloakroom but I'm also hearing you.

Offer Practical Help

Some churches have auto clinic days where single moms can bring their cars for tune-ups, oil changes or winterizing.

Other churches keep a file of handymen who are available to help around the house. Many of the churches wisely ask their men to go to the homes in teams of two.

Some churches have the well-meaning program of "Adopt a Family," but I don't want to be someone's Christian responsibility. I just want to be treated normally.

Simply invite us into your home just as you would any other family. And please accept when I invite your family to my home.

If my children are young, it would be great if you'd offer to take them shopping for my Christmas present.

Include My Children in Your Outings
The only "normal" family my children will see is yours. What a wonderful ministry you can have just by letting them join you for a family camp-out or church family night.

Jay has no idea what godly fathers do since he doesn't remember his dad. I'm praying already that his future father-in-law will like to talk about heavy issues and not just expect him to take part in hunting. One of our family jokes is "Ever been on a 'coon hunt, son?"

Talk to My Children
Even a two-minute conversation with my son in the hallway will make him look forward to coming to church. You don't have to include him with your family—though what a blessing that would be. But those few minutes each week will make him feel special.

I remember one man who gave 11-year-old Jay an electronic game. That was thoughtful, of course, but he didn't need a toy. He needed a man who would talk to him.

And don't discount the importance of just a few minutes. When I was 12 years old, the course of my life was changed in a five-minute meeting with my elderly neighbor's niece, Doris Schumacher. Doris taught English and social studies in Minneapolis and by her example showed me that education would be my key to a bright future.

You, too, can have that life-changing influence on another child.

Once More with Feeling

- Not only do we all need each other, but we all also need help.
- Ask the Lord for help and encouragement, but don't limit Him.
- The Lord can also send you help from many sources—from others He will direct to you, even your own kids.
- Get into a good church. The family of God is also your family. Even a few hours each week with other people who love the Lord will make a difference in your family.
- Involve the experts—teachers, counselors and even police—if you need help.
- Help usually comes only when we ask for it. So tell concerned people what you need—whether it's a need for specific prayer, instructions in tie-knotting, for adult conversation or for practical help.

TWELVE

COUNTING WRINKLES, CELEBRATING JOYS, ANTICIPATING LIFE

*"Teach us to number our days aright,
that we may gain a heart of wisdom."*
PSALM 90:12

On our tenth anniversary in 1976, I gave my husband the companion pictures of an old couple praying. I included a note that said, "Dearest Husband. May the Lord allow us to grow old together—and in His grace—like this dear old couple."

Even as I wrote it, I had an odd clutching within my spirit, as though I knew we'd never achieve that status together. But I shook the premonition off, afraid that thinking about it would make it come true.

Yes, I had planned for Don and me to grow old together, the way my grandparents did. But that didn't happen, and I have great chunks of memories I can't share with anyone, such as "Who was that couple who lived next door to us in married housing? The ones with the squeaky bed?"

But I'm carrying a dream again. Plenty of folks *are* growing old together and envying those of us who aren't married and who are growing old alone.

Accepting the Future

I learned to look for each day's joys the morning I found another streak of gray in my hair. And I learned it all from someone who at first glance didn't have anything to offer other than an empty seat in her breakfast booth.

Early that May 1987 Friday morning, I had peered into the mirror as I brushed back the hair from my face. The wing of gray at my right temple had widened almost overnight.

I tossed the brush onto the bathroom counter. It was definitely a day for breakfast at our favorite 1950s-style coffee shop.

The Coffee Shop in the middle of Mount Kisco, N.Y., is one of those narrow restaurants too busy serving breakfast to early morning workers to bother with the latest tile colors or soda machines. The five booths and dozen counter stools have witnessed almost 40 years of World Series arguments, weather complaints and social changes. Through it all the grill sizzled with over-easy eggs and plump hamburgers.

The counter stools were always occupied first, so we usually had no trouble getting a booth. That morning, however, even the booths were filled. We three stood by the door for a moment, surrounded by the combined smells of bacon grease, grilled bagels and strong coffee—wondering if anyone was about to leave.

Suddenly, an ancient woman in the back booth waved for us to join her. After our move from Michigan, we'd quickly learned that New Yorkers are used to sharing their space, so it wasn't an unusual invitation.

We smiled our thanks at the woman and walked toward her. Holly slid into the booth next to her, while Jay and I sat across from them. I thanked the woman for her kindness, then introduced myself and both teens.

She smiled and nodded, but merely pointed to her ear and shook her head. *Oh dear, she's deaf.*

We three sat uncomfortably silent, while our hostess continued with her breakfast. Her red, arthritic hands cut the poached egg on toast as I stared at my own hands, fearing (read "knowing") that someday they would look like hers.

Wasn't it enough that I'd found the new streak of gray just that morning? Did I need this second reminder of my mortality, too?

As I looked at Jay and Holly and flashed my standard "It's okay" smile, her hands still moved in my side vision. I forced my thoughts to other details of her person. The collar of her flowered navy blue dress peeked over the top of her tightly buttoned maroon sweater. Tinted glasses sat on the end of her nose.

Her hair was silver and covered by a bright blue winter cap. What color had her hair been? Nondescript brunette like mine? Or chestnut—its red highlights tossing bits of sunlight toward her admiring beau?

◆◆

Do I miss the smooth skin of my own youth? Of course. But do I *grieve* its loss? No, each line represents another milestone in my journey toward becoming the woman God wants me to be.

◆◆

Had her swollen hands once gently held babies who grew up and left for exotic places, remembering her only at Christmas and Mother's Day—if then? Had those same hands tenderly sponged the feverish forehead of an ill husband who, despite her care, died, leaving her to grow old alone?

She put her knife and fork across the plate, drank the last of the mug's weak coffee and then leaned toward Holly. "Why do you go to bed at night?" she asked.

Because we had thought she was probably mute as well as deaf, her question momentarily startled us. Finally Holly shrugged and answered, "Because I'm tired?"

The woman leaned forward, the sparkle in her eyes suddenly apparent. "Because the bed won't come to you!"

We three laughed appreciatively then, so she tapped the table surface in front of Jay. "If I put a quarter and a five-cent piece here, and the five-cent piece rolled off, why didn't the quarter roll off, too?"

Jay and I looked at each other in puzzlement. The woman smiled as she supplied the answer with obvious delight.

"Because the quarter has more sense!"

Her unexpected play on words was so comical that we all laughed. I waited for another riddle, but she busied herself, gathering up her newspaper and purse. Holly stood up to let her out of the booth.

She smiled at me, patted Holly's shoulder, gripped Jay's hand in farewell and was off—her head up and her stooped shoulders—momentarily, at least—straightened against the day.

The booth suddenly seemed empty. My immediate sense of loss was so evident that Holly asked, "What's wrong, Mom?"

I stared at her for a moment. True, what was wrong? Actually, nothing was wrong, but something was indeed gone. Yes, that was it—her joy. That dear, elderly woman had given us a moment of unexpected joy, a brief time of serendipity, and I wanted to relish it, for at least a little longer.

In those few moments we'd spent with her, I'd seen no self-pity, no laments for what she had lost and no admonishment that I enjoy these "best days of my life" with my children. She had merely invited us to share her private joy—and, in doing so, had shown us a more noble way to face challenges.

I smiled at the memory of her sparkling eyes. And that memory helped me accept the new gray streak in my hair as merely another well-earned milestone. *When I'm her age*, I told myself, *I hope I'm also teaching others to grab today's joy.*

And for now, I'll rejoice in what I have instead of lamenting what I've lost. And that's not a bad lesson to have learned so early in life.

Letting Go

If we've done our job right, our children won't want to stay around us forever. Oh, they'll enjoy coming home at the holidays, maybe, but for the most part, they'll go their own way. And that's supposed to be the end result of all of our parenting—to make them so strong that they will be able to take care of themselves.

So what do we do when they're gone—the very ones who have absorbed our time and thought for so long? We have to start thinking about that chapter in our lives long before it happens.

I've always enjoyed taking side trips. When Jay and Holly

were little, they went wherever I took them. By their early teens, they still went but complained a lot. In their midteens, I could get them to go only if I let each take a friend along.

Now we're to the point where they're usually involved in a church activity or sporting event, so if I want to go to a particular concert or special program, I go with *my* friends. I'm comfortable with that because we've done this in little steps along the way.

I don't want to be so dependent on my children that I can't function once they've left the nest. Nor do I want to whine, "Why don't you call me more often."

Of course, they won't call me as much as I'll wish, just as I didn't—and probably still *don't*—call my folks as much as they'd like. But if my two teens turn into mature, responsible adults, then I will have done my job well and, I trust, will be satisfied to wrap prayers around their little vessels as they sail off without me.

Planning Ahead

But in preparation for that coming day, I'm mentally adjusting to a schedule that will include things I like to do. For the first few weeks after they're both gone, I'll undoubtedly visit the local museums and tourist attractions Jay and Holly weren't interested in.

But I can handle that only so long. Eventually, I plan to devote my weekends to hospice work and studying for my next degree. I have to think of things to keep myself busy, so I won't drive my *adult* children nuts—after all, I concentrated on them for so many years!

But clutchy mothers actually drive adult children farther away. I want Jay and Holly to remain my friends long after they've stopped being my responsibility.

Most single mothers aren't to this place yet. They're still trying to find lost mittens and dropping the children off at the sitter's or juggling early teen schedules, worrying about unsupervised activities and trying to plan quality time. If you're one of those moms, "Hang in there!"

What you're going through now is absolutely exhausting, but your hard work will make the teen years so much easier. Your turn *is* coming when you can breathe at a normal rate again.

But even as I typed that last paragraph, I thought of the

old saying, "Just when a mother thinks her work is finished, she becomes a grandmother."

So we're in mothering for the long haul, but we have the challenge and joy of watching our loving influence make a difference in another's life. That's heady stuff.

Having Strength for Others

A few weeks ago, I watched the classic film *The Grapes of Wrath*. Perhaps because it was produced during the Great Depression when folks were desperate for hope, it ended on a happier note than the book did.

I was struck by the mother's incredible strength as she held her family together. She wasn't an attractive woman nor was she particularly sweet, but I liked her refusal to give up.

When the sky is caving in, someone must stand with arms thrust upward saying, "Here, come stand by me. It's going to be okay."

That's the type of woman I want to be.

Fighting for My Wrinkles

Now when I look in the mirror, I see a Titus 2:4 woman, someone who has the privilege of encouraging—and teaching—younger women.

Do I miss the smooth skin of my own youth? Of course.

But do I *grieve* its loss? No, each line represents another milestone in my journey toward becoming the woman God wants me to be.

Recently, I had my annual PR photo taken by a local studio. Since the prints were simple black-and-white 5" x 7"s, I expected them back within a few days. But when I called, the photographer said I couldn't have them for another week; she'd sent them to the finishing department to have the lines around my eyes airbrushed out.

"I don't want those lines brushed out," I said. "I've worked hard for them."

"But," she pointed out unnecessarily, "they make you look middle-aged."

"I *am* middle-aged," I declared. "Leave my wrinkles alone."

I refused to give in and the photos were ready for pickup

that afternoon. And, clearly, the wrinkles of years past were all there, unretouched and undiminished by cosmetic artifice.

Yes, every feature, every contour, every experience line was intact, each one a joyous witness to the years the Lord and I have walked in fellowship together; each one a precious reminder of the tears and joy shared with my beloved husband, Don; each one a powerful testimony to the love and devotion invested in my wonderful kiddos, Jay and Holly.

And these same lines are also harbingers of promise to the exciting adventures and fulfilling experiences that yet await me in the years ahead—perhaps as a speaker, a writer and editor, a mother-in-law, a grandmother, a whatever, but always—I trust—as the woman God wants me to be.

Once More with Feeling

- Don't waste energy by envying those couples growing old together. Plenty of marrieds growing old are envying us singles growing old alone.
- Accept the future by looking for the joys promised by each new day.
- Rejoice in what you have instead of lamenting what you've lost.
- Be ready to let go when the time comes. Of course, it's tough to let go of our children. But if we've done our job right, our children will be strong enough to go on without us.
- Plan ahead for the day when your children will be out of your nest and you will have time for those things you wanted to do.
- Remind yourself that your hectic schedule *now* will make the coming years that much easier. So for now, hang in there!
- You were strong for your children when they needed your strength. Even after they are gone and on their own, others will still be there who will need you to be strong for them.
- Accept the honor of being a Titus 2:4 woman—someone who has the privilege of teaching and encouraging younger women.
- And wear your wrinkles with pride. They are your badge of honor for all the years you have invested in your family.

New Adventures Are Ours to Grab. Let's Be Ready for Them!

*"'For I know the plans I have for you,'
declares the Lord, 'plans to prosper
you and not to harm you, plans to
give you hope and a future.'"*
JEREMIAH 29:11

We've all heard the saying, "When life hands you lemons, make lemonade!" One of my favorite stories illustrates that thought:

A church's new minister always left written instructions for his staff. A janitor who could not read or write was fired when he failed to respond to the written messages.

But instead of giving in to discouragement, the man began his own cleaning business and eventually became very wealthy.

One day, his banker was astounded when he discovered his customer's illiteracy. "Just imagine where you'd be if you could read and write!" he exclaimed.

The man smiled. "I'd be a janitor at the corner church."[1]

Know What You Truly Want

When you're faced with a major decision, remember the biblical three-step process: pray, read the Word and seek godly counsel. But what if you've done all that and you still don't have a clear answer?

When that happens to me, I know I'm probably fighting fear. In those moments, I ask myself *A year from now, what are you going to wish you had done?*

I've asked myself that twice—when we moved from Michigan to New York in 1986 and again in 1990 when we moved to Colorado. And both times, I've been glad I'd taken a deep breath and grabbed the adventure.

Maintain a Positive Attitude

Remember, in this life, we never get everything we want. For all of us, life is filled with trade-offs; for everything we lose, we gain something else. And for everything we gain, we lose.

That's why it is so important that we know what we truly want. And many times, our attitude decides the final outcome.

Discard Fear

In the summer of 1990, we were facing the move to Colorado Springs. I was convinced the Lord was offering me an incredible opportunity, and Jay wanted out of New York. There was only one hang-up: Holly's fears. How could I convince her she *would* survive?

Of course, I was praying constantly. Then one evening while Jay and Holly attended a youth activity, Doug and Lou Pardy, friends from church, invited me over for dinner. We chatted about parenting and our jobs, and Doug told about his work with the handicapped. One story he told offered the encouragement I needed.

As part of his training, Doug had worked in a hospital. A man had been there for several weeks recovering from an accident, but was still having trouble walking.

The doctors insisted this patient had no physical reason for the tiny, cautious steps he insisted upon, but he ignored their encouragement that he could do it. Then they assigned Doug to him.

The first afternoon with the man, Doug watched him take those fear-filled steps and then asked why he walked like that.

"I'm afraid I'll fall," the man replied.

I would have told the man, "You won't fall," but Doug merely asked another question:

"Did you ever fall when you were a kid."

"Sure, lots of times," the man said.

"Where?"

"On the grass."

Doug nodded and asked, "How about when you were older? Did you ever fall then?"

The man smiled. "Sure. I played softball. I was always falling, diving after a ball or for a base."

Doug nodded again. "Okay, we're going for a walk, and I'm going to trip you. You're going to fall. Then you're going to see that it was all right."

The man wasn't sure he could do that, but Doug coached him outside to the hospital lawn. As they walked along, Doug suddenly tripped him—just as he had promised he would do—and the man sprawled in the grass.

For a moment, he lay still, as though he was mentally checking for broken bones. Everything was okay. He stood up and grinned at Doug. Then he bounced up and down and even gave a little jump. He was going to be just fine.

That evening when I picked the kiddos up from the youth group, I put my arm around Holly and told the story.

Then I gave her an extra squeeze. "So, Honey, I'm going to trip you," I said. "But you're going to see that God is leading us, and that it's going to be okay."

She gave me one of her exasperated huffs, but she knew there would be no turning back. Now, these many months later, Holly admits that she really likes it here.

Whew!

Be Bold

In Tim Hansel's book, *Eating Problems for Breakfast*, he says, "Once you say, 'Yes, I can' (and really believe it), you'll be amazed at how much your problem-solving abilities will improve automatically. Your attitude must be one of boldness."[2]

He further reminds us that most of the psalms we find so uplifting were written during times of difficulty, and most of the epistles with their messages of joy and love were sent from prison. How's that for holy boldness?

My teaching buddy, Carl Amann, always kept this quotation on his board: "What happens isn't as important as how you react to it."

Yes, our attitude will make the difference in whether we're open to the good things God wants to give us. But often we get just what we expect out of life.

◆◆

We all have Jordan Rivers in our lives that we're afraid to cross. And, because we fear the risk and fail to cross, we are then unable to accept what the Lord offers us next.

◆◆

Years ago, I invited a perfectly healthy aunt to have dinner with us the following Thursday.

Her reply was simple: "Oh, I can't plan anything. I might be sick."

She missed numerous opportunities to have fun because she was afraid of taking a risk.

Have Courage

Years ago, I heard a minister say, "Courage is fear that has already said its prayers." I like that thought, for when we're afraid, we exaggerate our fears and say, "I'll never make it."

Do you recall the account in Numbers 13 when the spies returned from their survey of the Promised Land?

The fighters, like Caleb, said, "We *can* do it!"(see Num. 13:30).

But the tired ones lied, both to themselves and to the people, and said they couldn't possibly do it. "We seemed like grasshoppers in our own eyes, and we looked the same to them" (v. 33).

That's the way we feel when we're really up against it.

Remember that the sin is *not* in being afraid but in what we do with those fears.

Take Risks

I still remember the question my high school senior literature teacher, Mr. James LaGoe, posed to us:

"Who's more brave? The person who rushes to save another without thinking or the one who has time to consider it and still goes to the rescue?"

Even these years later, my answer is the same: "The one who knows what he's risking."

At one time or another, we all have Jordan Rivers in our lives that we're afraid to cross. And, because we fear the risk and fail to cross, we are then unable to accept what the Lord offers us next. When that happens, we end up living small pointless lives. Yet we really face no risk when we simply obey and go where the Lord leads.

What wonderful things we would experience if we claimed God's promises and starting looking at life boldly.

Keep a Merry Heart

In 1987, when Jay, Holly and I lived in New York, we ventured down to watch the Macy's Thanksgiving Day parade with friends—and with countless thousands of others. It was an incredible day of seeing the displays that had long been part of our holiday traditions, but only on TV. The best part of the day for me, though, was meeting a subway elevator operator.

For long hours each day he's trapped in that box under the streets of New York City and breathing air that's thick with dirt and fumes. I wouldn't have blamed him if he'd been grumpy and complained about being stuck underground. But he greeted us cheerfully and asked where we were from.

When he had delivered us to our requested level, he wished us well, asked us to come back again and added a cheerful, "I luv ya."

Later as we were waiting for the subway train on the lower level, we could hear him singing as he strolled in front of the elevator, waiting for his next batch of passengers. Rather than allowing himself to become embittered or discouraged by his lot in life, he chose to bring freshness, even joy to those who shared his day, even for those few moments.

So rather than fretting about our lot in life, let's become like that subway singer and give others reason to smile at our memory.

Waste No Time on Regrets

Regrets can keep us from accepting that bright new future, too. Years ago, I told Morrie Driesenga, my "Dutch papa," about my worry that I'd sold some furniture for too low a price.

His quick advice has since gotten me through more than mere furniture sales: "You've made your decision. Now live with it."

So even as we pray, we need to make a conscious effort to stop the "if onlys": "If only I hadn't moved," or "If only I hadn't taken that job."

A couple of summers ago, a friend was back in her hometown visiting relatives. While her children enjoyed a special outing with the cousins, she drove by the house where she had lived before her divorce. She felt almost as though she should pull into the driveway and honk the horn for her husband to help with the groceries.

But, of course, that was impossible, and she drove on with tears in her eyes. *Why didn't I have the good sense to enjoy those years instead of always looking for perfection?* she wondered.

Relief came only as she prayed, asking the Lord's forgiveness for not having appreciated His many blessings. And then she asked Him to help her start seeing the joy and preciousness of each new day. In that moment, she let go of the past and was willing to move forward.

Stay Thankful

In 1981, Chet Bitterman, Jr., a Wycliffe missionary in Bogota, Columbia, was kidnapped. For a long while, his father furiously paced his Pennsylvania home, wondering how he could rescue his son, when he suddenly heard within his spirit, "Give thanks."

To give thanks was the last thing Chet, Sr. wanted to do. He'd already given serious thought to rounding up an armed group of his friends, flying into the South American city and taking it apart, brick by brick.

The Act of Giving Thanks

But as he struggled with the Spirit's witness in his heart, he realized the command was to *give* thanks, not *feel* thanks. As he wondered what he could possibly be thankful *for*, he remembered that his son had memorized hundreds of Scripture verses.

Surely those verses are encouraging him right now, he thought. And he immediately gave thanks for the reassurance and courage that the Word of God was giving Chet, Jr. at that very moment.

The Benefit of Giving Thanks

Upon further reflection, Chet, Sr. added further thankfulness for his son's physical strength and emotional stability. The list grew. When young Chet's body was found in an abandoned bus 48 days later, the spirit of thankfulness already sown enabled his father to open his heart now to the comfort the Lord wanted to give him.

Remembering that account has helped me often in this life of singlehood that was thrust upon me years ago when my husband died. For I decided that if Chet, Sr. could find something to be thankful for in the midst of his great emotional pain, surely I could, too. And I have done just that, many, many times. And I trust I will continue to find many more.

The Attitude of Giving Thanks

A thankful attitude enables us to live life with joy and to rejoin life when we feel momentarily estranged from it. More than that, having a thankful spirit enables us to laugh and love with genuine abandon. For without thankfulness, we would wither within and be in danger of becoming bitter, mirthless creatures, a drag on ourselves and everyone around us.

So rejoice and give thanks. If you haven't found something today to give thanks for, you haven't looked very hard. If you need some help in that department, consider these three simple suggestions from writer/editor Elizabeth

Sherrill that are guaranteed to make every day a day of thanksgiving:

1. Every day, surprise someone with a thank-you.
2. Every day, thank God for something you have never until now thanked Him for.
3. Every day thank God for something about which you are not now happy.[3]

Practice them, yes, even when you don't feel like giving thanks! The ongoing act will in itself return the spirit of thankfulness and thanksgiving to you.

So try it. You'll like it. I know.

Be Open to the Lord's Blessings

Keeping my life open to the Lord's blessings is a lesson I especially needed as a single mother—but one I had to learn the hard way.

The Opportunity

In 1978, I met Marta Gabre-Tsadick, the first woman senator of Ethiopia, at a Michigan conference grounds. Her very stance announced authority and grace. Stately and beautiful, she was everything I wasn't.

My pastor, who was at the same conference that week, knew of Marta's renown and invited her to tell our church about the Marxist takeover in 1974 of her beloved Ethiopia—the world's oldest Christian nation.

Impulsively, I asked Marta to stay with my family the weekend she would speak. She accepted, and I assumed the matter was settled.

The Self-doubt

Several weeks later, however, a friend who had visited Marta's home commented that Marta had served her a glass of water from a tray. Outwardly, I nodded at how much that sounded like the gracious Marta. But inwardly, I cringed.

Serving a glass of water from a tray? I couldn't remember if I owned a tray, let alone if I knew how to serve from it. At our home, if someone comes into the kitchen and asks for a drink of water, I'm apt to continue whatever I'm doing and wave toward the cabinets.

"Sure. The glasses are up there. The water's in the refrigerator. Help yourself."

So what in the world was I thinking of when I decided to invite someone like *Marta* into my home?

As the days passed, I became more tense. I considered buying a tray and practicing with it. However, the thought of stumbling and dumping the water into her lap changed my mind.

My self-imposed misery continued. I even thought of writing to Marta and saying a crisis had forced me to withdraw my offer and that we'd provide a motel room instead. No, my statement wouldn't be a lie—my inner turmoil had already resulted in several sleepless nights.

◆◆

Ask, seek and knock are words of action for us. Even as much as we long to be rescued from problems, we still are responsible for the results. The Lord has promised to help us, to direct us, but we still have to take that first step in faith.

◆◆

The Petition

Finally, I did what I should have done when the trauma first started—I prayed. As I poured out my insecurities, I knew God already understood my problem, but I needed to hear myself being honest.

I described the contrast between my background and Marta's and listed all the reasons why I couldn't possibly have such a dignified woman in *my* home. Then I had the good sense to shut up and listen.

The Release

The room wasn't suddenly filled with a golden light, and no trumpet blast heralded a message. But a deep calm settled over me. It was just as though the Lord was saying, "Marta is doing a good job at being Marta. Now you must do equally well at being who you are."

Freedom rushed in. We'd had guests before; I'd just haul

out my best company recipes and invite my pastor and his wife over, too, to help carry the conversation.

The Fellowship

When the appointed weekend arrived, Marta, her husband, Deme, and their two sons proved to be such delightful guests that I found myself concentrating on the exciting story of their miraculous escape from Ethiopia rather than on myself.

Afterward, Marta offered to help with the dishes, but I insisted she leave them for me. I urged her to rest instead before speaking that evening.

Reluctantly, she left the kitchen as I cleared the counter. But, in a few minutes, she was back.

"May I please have a glass of water?" she asked in her softly accented voice.

Without thinking, I answered, "Sure. The glasses are in that cabinet, and the water's in the refrigerator. Help yourself."

The words were barely out of my mouth when embarrassment swept over me. How could I have spoken like that to Marta, of all people. I know God had reminded me to be myself, but this was going too far. I bit my lip in frustration.

The Blessing

That night, as we prepared to leave for the church, Marta gave me a special hug. Then, with her hand on the doorknob, she suddenly turned back to me. Tears were in her eyes.

"Thank you for making us feel so much at home here. For two years we have not felt part of a family until now."

She paused, then shared her great hurt. "We had to leave our families behind—our parents and brothers. Thank you for allowing us to be part of *your* family. Thank you for letting me get my own water."

By then, I was crying, too, but with joy. I had almost allowed my insecurities to rob me of an incredible blessing.

And Move out in Faith

With the Lord's help—and as we ask Him to bring His good out of our pain—we can do more than merely survive our situation; we can actually be victorious over it.

But we can't get arrogant about our ability to face the challenges ahead. I learned that when we were still living in Michigan.

John and Elizabeth Sherrill had invited me out to Chappaqua, New York, to talk about a writing project. I was elated—and nervous as a cat.

New York was the end of the world to me then. How could I possibly fly to LaGuardia Airport, rent a car and drive the hour north on those mysterious eastern parkways? But John sent me a map as though he was confident of my ability to handle such a huge challenge.

The plane landed safely, and I picked up the rental car. I studied my map that, if I followed it correctly, would lead me through the area around LaGuardia until I could pick up the route to head north.

Pray—a Lot

And I prayed constantly: "Well, Lord, you know I have the worst sense of direction of anybody in the world. But I trust you to guide me and get me there safely and back to the airport on time."

With a giant sigh, I put the car into gear and started out through the gate. At each stoplight, I reexamined the map.

Which way, Lord?

Amazingly, at every turn I just knew the way to go. At one point, the street sign had been knocked down. I cocked my head to decipher the way it had been pointing, but it was as though He was sitting right at my elbow, saying, "Turn left at the next stop."

It was an amazing day. Not only did I spend the day with the Sherrills, but I drove through New York City— both miracles for a Harlan County, Kentucky, gal.

Let Him Take It from Here

My plane back home landed at Detroit's Metro Airport right on time. I was 20 minutes from home and would drive a route I'd driven dozens of times. As I located my car in the parking lot, I didn't *say* it, but my attitude was one of "Thanks, God. Now I'll take it from here!"

An hour later, with my frustration growing by the minute, I was still trying to get off Ecorse Road. It wasn't until I prayed again, asking for help that I finally got onto I-94 and headed home.

Since then I've often found myself praying, "Don't let me take it from here again. *Your* will only."

I learned that night I can't always handle the most familiar things, so I have to trust the unfamiliar to Him, too. But I've also learned He wants to help us get back on the right road—if we'll let Him.

Ask, Seek, Knock

Because I am God's child, He is concerned about every aspect of my life. I like those three verbs in Luke 11:9: "*Ask* and it will be given to you; *seek* and you will find; *knock* and the door will be opened to you."

Ask, seek and knock are words of action for us. Even as much as we long to be rescued from problems, we still are responsible for the results. The Lord has promised to help us, to direct us, but we still have to take that first step in faith.

He's standing by us, waiting for us to ask Him to help us juggle all our scary responsibilities. And as we do, we will find that wonderful experiences *are* ahead for us—if we'll just allow the Lord to give them to us.

Once More with Feeling

- When life hands you lemons, make lemonade.
- Know what you truly want out of life, because no one gets everything he wants. That's why life is full of trade-offs.
- When you're faced with a major decision, remember the biblical three-step process: pray, read the Word and seek godly counsel.
- When you're fighting fear, ask yourself, *A year from now, what will I wish I had done?*
- When you make a decision, your attitude often decides the final outcome. So maintain a positive attitude toward life.
- Put aside your fears and, with boldness and courage, be ready to take some risks.
- What happens isn't as important as how you react to it.

- Keep a merry heart and give others reason to smile at the memory of you.
- Waste no time on regrets. Instead, let go of the past and ask God to help you see the joy and preciousness of each new day.
- Always give thanks, even when you don't feel thankful. The act renews a spirit of thankfulness within.
- Don't allow your insecurities to rob you of the incredible blessings God has in store for you.
- With the Lord's help—and as we ask Him to bring His good out of our pain—we can do more than merely survive our situation; we can actually be victorious over it.
- Remember, in Christ, you are God's child, and He is concerned about every aspect of your life. He has promised to help you, so ask, seek and knock in faith.

Notes

1. A. Philip Parham, *Letting God: Christian Meditations for Recovering Persons* (New York: HarperCollins Publishers, 1987), reading for March 30.
2. Tim Hansel, *Eating Problems for Breakfast* (Dallas, TX: Word, Inc., Word Books, 1988), p. 26.
3. Elizabeth Sherrill, *Journey into Rest* (Minneapolis, MN: Bethany House, 1990), pp. 158-160.

SUPPORT GROUPS
FOR FAMILIES

T he Lord takes care of our needs, but sometimes He chooses to do that through organizations. If you want a support group for yourself and your family, look first to the local church. Small congregations can offer a needed sense of family; larger ones often offer divorce recovery workshops, grief seminars, expanded youth programs and various singles ministries.

But if you or a family member have a specific need beyond what you think the local church can meet, here are some folks to contact:

Alcoholics for Christ
1316 North Campbell Road
Royal Oak, MI 48067
1-800-441-7877

An evangelical fellowship
for substance abusers and their
families.

**Association of Christian
Conciliation Services**
1537 Avenue D, Suite 352
Billings, MT 59102
406-256-1583

An organization that helps

resolve disputes before a panel
of believers.

Christian Helplines, Inc.
P.O. Box 10117
Tampa, FL 33679
813-251-4040

A suicide/crisis prevention
ministry.

Christian Horizons
P.O. Box 334
Williamston, MI 48895
517-655-3463

A ministry to the mentally
handicapped.

Concerned Women of America
370 L'Enfant Promenade, Suite 800
Washington, D.C. 20024
1-800-458-8797

A prayer and action group that aims at protecting the rights and interests of the family.

Crisis Pregnancy Centers
Christian Action Council
701 W. Broad Street, Suite 405
Falls Church, VA 22046
703-237-2100

An evangelical outreach to women with problem pregnancies.

Exodus International
P.O. Box 2121
San Rafael, CA 94912-2121
415-454-1017

A clearinghouse for ministries to those families and individuals affected by homosexuality.

Family Research Council
700 13th St. NW
Washington, D.C. 20005
202-393-2100

A division of Focus on the Family that encourages emphasis on traditional Judeo-Christian values within the government.

Fellowship of Christian Athletes
8701 Leeds Road
Kansas City, MO 64129
816-921-0909

A Bible-based ministry for coaches and students.

Focus on the Family
Colorado Springs, CO 80993

An evangelical ministry stressing traditional family values.

Joni and Friends
P.O. Box 948
Agoura Hills, CA 91301
818-707-5664

A ministry to the physically disabled.

Josh McDowell Ministry
P.O. Box 1000
Dallas, TX 75221
214-907-1000

A ministry geared to teens that encourages them to resist sexual pressures of society and their peers.

Life After Assault League, Inc.
1336 W. Lindbergh
Appleton, WI 54914
414-739-4489

A service providing counseling for the sexually abused.

Love Inc. Church Services Networks
P.O. Box 1616
Holland, MI 49422
616-392-8277

Love, Inc. matches needs of those requiring assistance with local church resources.

Moms in Touch
P.O. Box 1120
Poway, CA 92074-1120
619-486-4065

A prayer group of mothers of public school students.

MOPS
4175 Hadan St. Suite 105
Wheat Ridge, CO 80033
303-420-6100

An evangelical group for
mothers of preschoolers.

Neighborhood Bible Study
P.O. Box 222
Dobbs Ferry, NY 10522
914-693-3273

A group providing help for
starting adult Bible studies.

**New Life
Treatment Centers, Inc.**
570 Glenneyre #107
Laguna Beach, CA 92651
1-899-227-LIFE
1-800-332-TEEN (hotlines)
714-494-8383 (office)

These centers provide
Christian psychiatric care.

Open Arms
P.O. Box 1056
Columbia, MO 65205
314-449-7672

Open Arms offers help to
those suffering from the
aftermath of abortion.

Overcomers Outreach
2290 W. Whittier Blvd.
La Habra, CA 90631
213-697-3994

Support groups for the chem-
ically dependent and their
families.

Respect Inc.
P.O. Box 349
Bradley, IL 60915
815-932-8389

This organization stresses sex
education with a Christian
emphasis.

Salvation Army
National Headquarters
799 Bloomfield Ave.
Verona, NJ 07044
201-239-0606

Spiritual counseling and
material assistance offered.
Look in the white pages of your
telephone directory for the
branch nearest you.

Single Adult Ministries
4540 15th Avenue, N.E.
Seattle, WA 98105
206-524-7300

An outreach to mature singles.

Social Services
Local offices are usually listed in
the "County" section of your
telephone directly. See such list-
ings as "Public Health Services"
and "Public Social Services
Agency." The many services
available include financial aid,
food stamps, resources for emergency needs, adult education,
day care and housing.

Teen-Aid
North 1330 Calispel
Spokane, WA 99201
509-328-2080

Provides educational materials
encouraging abstinence.

Teen Challenge
1525 N. Campbell Avenue
Springfield, MO 65803
417-862-6969

A Christian youth ministry that includes programs for drug and alcohol treatment.

Women's Aglow Fellowship
P.O. Box 1548
Lynnwood, WA 98046-1556
206-775-7282

A charismatic Christian community outreach ministry for women.

Young Life
P.O. Box 520
Colorado Springs, CO 80901
719-473-4262

A Christian youth ministry for teens in high school.

Youth for Christ
Youth Guidance Division
360 Main Place
Carol Stream, IL 60188

A nondenominational ministry that works with youth. Campus Life Clubs reach out to mainstream high school students. The Youth Guidance program works with troubled youth. Programs include a summer camp ministry. Check the white pages of your phone directory to contact Youth for Christ in your area.

The author expresses special thanks to *Christian Herald* magazine of Chappaqua, New York, for permission to include many of these names and addresses from its *1991 Christian Action Guide*.

RECOMMENDED READING FOR SINGLE MOMS

H ere are a few books you may find helpful. I've included some of my favorites that don't deal specifically with single parenting, but they do touch on many of the personal issues that can influence our relationship to our children.

Check with your Christian bookstore for more titles.

Adams, J. E. *From Forgiven to Forgiving.* Wheaton, IL: Victor Books, 1989.

Aldrich, Sandra P. *Living Through the Loss of Someone You Love.* Ventura, CA: Regal Books, 1990.

Arterburn, Stephen and Jim Burns. *Drug Proof Your Kids.* Pomona, CA: Focus on the Family, 1989.

Authelet, Dr. Emil. *Parenting Solo: How to Enjoy Life and Raise Good Kids.* San Bernardino, CA: Here's Life Publishers, Inc., 1989.

Barnes, Robert G., Jr. *Single Parenting: A Wilderness Journey.* Wheaton, IL: Tyndale House, 1984.

Blue, Ron. *The Debt Squeeze: How Your Family Can Become Financially Free.* Pomona, CA: Focus on the Family, 1989.

Briles, Judith. *Money Guide for Christian Women.* Ventura, CA: Regal Books, 1991.

Burkett, Larry. *Answers to Your Family's Financial Questions*. Pomona, CA: Focus on the Family, 1987.
—————. *The Complete Financial Guide for Single Parents*. Wheaton, IL: Victor Books, 1991.

Burnham, Sue. *Living with Your Emotions*. Wheaton, IL: Tyndale House, 1989.

Chesser, Beverly. *Beverly Exercise—Your Health Coach*. Springdale, PA: Whitaker House, 1988.

Cook, Barbara. *Love and Its Counterfeits*. Lynnwood, WA: Aglow Publications, 1989.

Crabb, Dr. Lawrence. *Inside Out*. Colorado Springs, CO: NavPress, 1988.

Dobson, Dr. James. *Dare to Discipline*. Wheaton, IL: Tyndale House, 1973.
—————. *Dr. Dobson Answers Your Questions About Raising Children*. Wheaton, IL: Tyndale House, 1982.
—————. *Emotions: Can You Trust Them?* Ventura, CA: Regal Books, 1984.
—————. *Love Must Be Tough*. Irving, TX: Word, Inc., Word Books, 1983.
—————. *Parenting Isn't for Cowards*. Irving, TX: Word, Inc., Word Books, 1987.
—————. *Preparing for Adolescence*. rev. ed. Ventura, CA: Regal Books, 1989.
—————. *The Strong-Willed Child*. Wheaton, IL: Tyndale House, 1978.

Duin, Julia. *Purity Makes the Heart Grow Stronger: Sexuality and the Single Christian*. Ann Arbor, MI: Servant Publications, Vine Books, 1988.

Foehner, Charlotte and Carol Cozart. *The Widow's Handbook: A Guide for Living*. Golden, CO: Fulcrum, Inc., 1987.

Hansel, Tim. *Holy Sweat*. Irving, TX: Word, Inc., Word Books, 1987.
—————. *You Gotta Keep Dancin'*. Elgin, IL: David C. Cook Publishing Co., 1985.

Hosier, Helen. *The Thinking Christian Woman*. Eugene, OR: Harvest House Publishers, Inc., 1988.

Johnson, Barbara. *Fresh Elastic for Stretched-Out Moms*. Old Tappan, NJ: Fleming H. Revell Co., 1985.

Kent, Carol. *Secret Passions of the Christian Woman*.

Colorado Springs, CO: NavPress, 1990.

Lee, Dr. Peter. *Straight Talk About Sex.* Old Tappan, NJ: Fleming H. Revell Co., 1989.

LeSourd, Sandra Simpson. *The Compulsive Woman.* Old Tappan, NJ: Fleming H. Revell Co., Chosen Books, 1987.

Linamen, Karen Scalf and Linda Holland. *The Curious Waltz of the Working Woman: Finding Your Personal Rhythm in the Dance Between Family, Work and Friends.* Ventura, CA: Regal Books, 1990.

Lush, Jean and Pamela Vredevelt. *Mothers and Sons: Raising Boys to Be Men.* Old Tappan, NJ: Fleming H. Revell Co., 1988.

MacDonald, Gordon. *Rebuilding Your Broken World.* Nashville, TN: Thomas Nelson Publishers, 1988.

McDowell, Josh. *How to Help Your Child Say "No" to Sexual Pressure.* Irving, TX: Word, Inc., Word Books, 1987.

──────. *Teens Speak Out: What I Wish My Parents Knew About Sexuality.* San Bernardino, CA: Here's Life Publishers, Inc., 1987.

Marshall, Catherine. *To Live Again.* New York: Avon Books, 1976.

Merrill, Dean. *Another Chance: How God Overrides Our Big Mistakes.* Grand Rapids, MI: Zondervan Publishing House, 1981.

Merrill, Dean and Grace. *Together at Home: One Hundred Proven Activities to Nurture Your Children's Faith.* Pomona, CA: Focus on the Family, 1988.

Mowday, Lois. *Daughters Without Dads.* Nashville, TN: Thomas Nelson Publishers, 1990.

──────. *The Snare: Avoiding Emotional and Sexual Entanglements.* Colorado Springs, CO: NavPress, 1988.

O'Connor, Lindsey. *Working at Home: A Dream That's Becoming a Trend.* Eugene, OR: Harvest House Publishers, Inc., 1990.

Reed, Bobbie. *Single Mothers Raising Sons.* Nashville, TN: Thomas Nelson Publishers, 1988.

Richmond, Gary. *Successful Single Parenting.* Eugene, OR: Harvest House Publishers, Inc., 1989.

Schmidt, Kenneth A. *Finding Your Way Home: Freeing the Child Within You and Discovering Wholeness in the*

Functional Family of God. Ventura, CA: Regal Books, 1990.

Sell, Charles. *Unfinished Business: Helping Adult Children Resolve Their Past.* Portland, OR: Multnomah Press, 1989.

Sherrill, Elizabeth. *Journey into Rest.* Minneapolis, MN: Bethany House, 1991.

Smith, Hannah Whitall. *God Is Enough.* New York: Random House, Ballantine Books, 1990.

Smith, Harold Ivan. *Positively Single.* Wheaton, IL: Victor Books, 1986.

—————. *Single and Feeling Good.* Nashville, TN: Abingdon Press, 1987.

Smith, Virginia W. *The Single Parent: Revised, Updated and Expanded.* Old Tappan, NJ: Fleming H. Revell Co., Power Books, 1983.

Sneed, Dr. David and Dr. Sharon Sneed. *Prime Time: A Health Guide for Women Over Forty.* Irving, TX: Word, Inc., Word Books, 1989.

Swindoll, Charles R. *For Those Who Hurt.* Portland, OR: Multnomah Press, 1977.

Thoene, W. Brock. *Protecting Your Income and Your Family's Future.* Minneapolis, MN: Bethany House, 1989.

Weber, Ellen. *Single, but Not Alone.* Nashville, TN: Broadman Press, 1990.

Whelchel, Mary. *Common Mistakes Singles Make.* Old Tappan, NJ: Fleming H. Revell Co., 1989.

White, John. *Parents in Pain.* Downers Grove, IL: InterVarsity Press, 1979.

Wright, H. Norman. *Always Daddy's Girl: Understanding Your Father's Impact on Who You Are.* Ventura, CA: Regal Books, 1989.

—————. *The Power of a Parent's Words.* Ventura, CA: Regal Books, 1991.

Young, Helen and Billie Silvey. *Time Management for Christian Women.* Grand Rapids, MI: Zondervan Publishing House, 1990.